Praise for

LEVERAGING THE UNIVERSE

**Testimonials for the audio program of the same title
that inspired this book**

"I wondered how you could possibly add to *Infinite Possibilities*.
Now I know!"

"If I had to give my children ONLY ONE thing to
listen to in the world, it would be your information
about leveraging the Universe."

"I just wanted to let you know that after listening to *Leveraging
the Universe*, I finally pulled myself out of a severe depression that
had me giving serious thought to suicide. Years of docs, meds,
and other stuff didn't do the trick, but listening to you flipped
some sort of switch in my brain, and now life is just SO MUCH
BETTER. Words can hardly express my gratitude,
but I had to let you know."

"Fun story, Mike: I had your CD playing in my car when I
loaned it to a friend. Later, she just had to know what was playing
on my radio! A couple of days after that, I took my car in for
repair, and the mechanic called me, and he said, 'Before we talk
about your estimate, I want to know who's talking on your CDs!'"

"You speak in a much more pragmatic way than anyone I have *ever* heard."

"I think your teachings should be mandatory for people who are moving from thinking in the 'old camp' into 'new thought.' You make it clear what we *must* do in the physical and what we can leave to the Universe."

"Perfect for anyone who feels at all stuck or limited in any way!"

"I feel like a huge weight has been lifted off my shoulders . . . a sense of peace that I haven't felt in ages. Thanks, Mike!"

"You totally blew me away! I am in awe with the material you presented!"

"Have been listening to your *Leveraging the Universe* CDs for the last two days while driving from town to town in our beautiful Queensland, the 'Sunshine State' of Australia. I'm stoked and just love the analogies you use to explain things that I have heard before but could never quite grasp."

"MIKE!! OMG OMG OMG!!!"

"I just purchased *Leveraging the Universe*—absolutely fantastic!! I get to learn, I get to smile and laugh, I get the essential tools I was missing—and the dots are connecting. I am forever grateful for your presence, your inspirations, your willingness to share. Thank you!"

"My adult daughter suffers from mental illness. Last year she was also diagnosed with MS and diabetes. That whammy really put her in a downward spiral. A month ago, she started listening to *Leveraging the Universe*. I cannot tell you what a CHANGE it has made! No medication or therapy has made the difference you have! It's wonderful to have my beautiful daughter back."

"Your arguments are cogent; your personality is endearing; and your approach is of a good friend, not a guru . . . You left me uplifted."

"I finally have a tool to explain everything within my own mind. Your analogies about life and the Universe are remarkable. I have thought along the same lines as you for over a decade, but to find another voice explaining it all the way you have is extremely liberating. Using these principles, I am in the job that I have always wanted (at the envy of most), engaged to be married to the girl of my dreams, in the house that I envisioned over ten years ago, running a successful business of my own, in the pursuit of financial freedom, and I have family and friends who respect me for who I am. I do not expect a reply—just [want] you to know that I exist and appreciate your sharing."

"What I had not thought about or anticipated was the marvelous gift of your giving information in such a way that I was not left with a sense of 'Mike Dooley is great, but I can't do those things.' You have an ability to share your experiences in a way that makes the material come alive without drawing energy to yourself. So I want to say thank you very, very much for that."

"Mike, you've made an incredible difference in my life. *Leveraging the Universe* helped me create an incredibly successful real estate investment company by helping me take the first step on 'my side of the triangle' and 'untie the boat from the dock.' You also helped me be positive enough to save my daughter's nosedive into depression after losing three children . . . she's good now. And you gave me the strength to save my marriage— my husband is AMAZING!"

"Before *Leveraging the Universe*, I was already reading some books about visualizing and the Universe being inside of me, but those books were somewhat vague. Thanks to your explanations, and the easy seven steps, I finally understand what I'm reading."

"WOW. I love how you've simplified universal truths! I simply do not know how to thank you enough."

"You are such a BRILLIANT BEING OF LIGHT. You radiate LOVE and TRUTH. Every word you spoke was a truth that I already knew, and you brought many neglected passages to the surface for me—'tis odd how easily we can forget!"

"Thanks for the practical tools to refine my creative powers, bringing into my life more of what I want and less of what I fear."

"Wow! Your passion, insights, and sharing of your own experiences are so inspiring!"

Leveraging the
UNIVERSE

Also by Mike Dooley

Notes from the Universe

More Notes from the Universe

Even More Notes from the Universe

Choose Them Wisely

Infinite Possibilities

Manifesting Change

Audio Books

Leveraging the Universe and Engaging the Magic

2012: Prophecies and Possibilities

Leveraging the
UNIVERSE

7 Steps to Engaging Life's Magic

Mike Dooley

Author of the *New York Times* bestseller
Infinite Possibilities

ATRIA PAPERBACK
New York London Toronto Sydney New Delhi

BEYOND WORDS
Portland, Oregon

ATRIA PARASENBACK
A Division of Simon & Schuster, Inc.
1230 Avenue of the Americas
New York, NY 10020

BEYOND WORDS
1750 S.W. Skyline Blvd., Suite 20
Portland, Oregon 97221-2543
503-531-8700 / 503-531-8773 fax
www.beyondword.com

Managing editor: Lindsay S. Brown
Editor: Julie Clayton
Copyeditor: Henry Covey
Proofreader: Jade Chan
Design: Devon Smith
Composition: William H. Brunson Typography Services

First Atria Books/Beyond Words trade paperback edition November 2012

ATRIA PAPERBACK and colophon are trademarks of Simon & Schuster, Inc.
Beyond Words Publishing is an imprint of Simon & Schuster, Inc., and the Beyond Words logo is a registered trademark of Beyond Words Publishing, Inc.

For more information about special discounts for bulk purchases, please contact Simon
& Schuster Special Sales at 1-866-506-1949 or business@simonandschuster.com.

The Simon & Schuster Speakers Bureau can bring authors to your live event.
For more information or to book an event, contact the Simon & Schuster Speakers
Bureau at 1-866-248-3049 or visit our website at www.simonspeakers.com.

Manufactured in the United States of America

10 9 8 7 6 5 4 3 2 1

The Library of Congress has cataloged the hardcover edition as follows:

Dooley, Mike.
    Leveraging the universe : 7 steps to engaging life's magic / Mike Dooley.
        p.   cm.
        1. New Thought.   2. Self-realization.   3. Success.   4. Self-help techniques.
    I. Title.
    BF632.D672   2011
    158—dc23
                                                    2011022578

ISBN: 978-1-58270-314-5 (hc)
ISBN: 978-1-58270-315-2 (pbk)
ISBN: 978-1-4516-3391-7 (ebook)

The corporate mission of Beyond Words Publishing, Inc.: *Inspire to Integrity*

To Marisol

CONTENTS

CONTENTS

PREFACE

The content of this book originated as the material I delivered during my first world tour in 2003 and 2004, shortly after I released the audio program *Infinite Possibilities: The Art of Living Your Dreams*. At the time, *Infinite Possibilities* was more of an academic A–Z offering of the workings of all "things" time and space, but it became apparent that my follow-up work, which was to be delivered face-to-face before audience members, would ideally offer a practical way of immediately *applying* what I had shared in *Infinite Possibilities*. "Leveraging the Universe: Engaging the Magic" was the name I gave to this application-oriented material gathered from my tour, and it was subsequently released as a live audio recording. Finally, it became the book that's now in your hands.

Leveraging the Universe: 7 Steps to Engaging Life's Magic creates a bridge for those still immersed in old-school methodologies of changing their lives, such as simple goal setting and positive thinking, and offers some new-school approaches to consider, using an objective, sequential approach to harnessing life's magic and the innate supernatural powers within us all. All too often, the "old schoolers" think they must go it alone, be in the right place, know all the right people, and succeed by the sweat of their brows while they inadvertently carry the weight of the world on their shoulders.

At the other end of the spectrum are the "new schoolers," who've read all the books, done all the workshops, and concluded that they need do nothing other than surrender to a loving, conspiring Universe so that their lives might be transformed by its magic—though they silently wonder why their lives haven't changed.

The answer lies somewhere between the two, which effectively means learning the difference between what we can, should, and must do for ourselves and what we can, should, and must delegate to the metaphysical principles that have been around since the dawn of time. Our part is the easy part. We need only to hoist our sails so that they can then be filled with life's magical winds. Yet without offering token efforts and taking baby steps in the direction of our dreams, not only do we contradict our desire to live as fully as possible but we also slide ever further away from an infinite grace that tirelessly strives to sweep us off our feet, surround us with friends, and create the life we want most.

Leveraging is about using the gifts of thought, word, and deed to harness this grace. It's about doing the least to get the most. It's about learning the truth and then living it so that the kingdom, the power, and the glory can be revealed before your very eyes—as you discover your holy place in creation as a creator yourself.

Throughout this book, I'll walk you through various stories, explanations, and anecdotes, some of which I draw from my early works because they're so critically important. I'll clearly explain:

* The availability of the Universe's profound power
* How to get it working for you
* All that you can have, do, and be

In addition, I'll occasionally draw parallels to my own experiences, since I used these very lessons to sort out the seeming "train wreck" of my own life eleven years ago, illustrating the steps that anyone can take to "get their groove back on."

Slayer of dragons, matador of time and space, rightful heir to heaven on earth, it's time to begin living the life of *your* dreams.

Your great admirer,

INTRODUCTION

A s I've recounted in earlier works, the first time I can remember actually leveraging life's magic, quite accidentally, was as a nine-year-old boy, fresh from a horseback riding competition in which I placed sixth (out of six). Determined to do better, and following my mother's sage advice, I prayed to God each night to "help me do my best" in the next competition. Nightly I prayed, *imagining myself as the next champion*, and those thoughts rather promptly became a first-place trophy.

I first *intentionally* leveraged life's magic to save myself from losing my job at Price Waterhouse (now PricewaterhouseCoopers) due to my total and utter incompetence. Just weeks into a practice of visualizing every day, seeing myself happy at work (even though I was absolutely miserable), I was suddenly whisked into the company's tax department, and my career took off like a space shuttle.

With this success of deliberately turning my thoughts into things, I decided to enhance the process by creating my first scrapbook (much like today's vision boards) as a tool to help me visualize the details of my dreamed-of life. In it, I pasted pictures from magazines of all the things I wanted: a fancy car, a condo, a house, and so forth. And I included pictures of foreign destinations that, one day, I might visit: London, Paris, Hong Kong, and Tokyo.

Two years later, no one was more surprised than I that I was living abroad in the Middle East on a two-year assignment for the firm. One fine morning while having breakfast at the Regent Hotel in Kowloon, Hong Kong, in transit to the United States on my first home leave, my heart nearly skipped a beat when I looked up over my coffee and out the two-story plate-glass windows surrounding me to suddenly realize that I was sitting before the exact same view of Hong Kong Island that I had cut and pasted into my little scrapbook just twenty-four months earlier.

When my assignment in the Middle East was finished, I received my first choice of cities to repatriate to: Boston, Massachusetts. There I bought my dream condo, so close to downtown that I walked to work every day. Eighteen months later, I decided to quit my job to pursue another dream—to become an entrepreneur. Selling my condo for seed money, I moved to Orlando, Florida, and quickly teamed up with my brother, Andy, a graphic artist, and my mother, Sheelagh, who's really cool, and we launched TUT Enterprises, Inc. (TUT for "Totally Unique T-shirts"). We put my brother's art, combined with my thoughts and poems about life, dreams, and happiness, on shirts, gifts, greeting cards, key chains, and posters. In the decade that followed, the three of us grossed more than $10 million in sales around the world.

And then—the "train wreck."

In spite of the emotional carnage at the time of my "train wreck" (which really wasn't a train wreck), it's odd how the calamity now seems like a hazy memory from a distant "past life." In fact, as I revisit those times in order to tell you my story, which I'll recount from time to time in the chapters that follow, it brings back forgotten "nightmares" that seem almost impossible for me to believe were once mine, because within twenty-four months of the seeming derailment, I was the author of one of the hottest-selling self-improvement audio programs in the world. Twelve months after that, I had already begun a world tour that would deliver this very material. And twenty-four months after that, I was featured in the international film and book phenomenon *The Secret*. Since then, while many more wonderful things have happened, the professional achievement that has meant the most to me was when *Infinite Possibilities* debuted on the *New York Times* bestsellers list.

Yet even better than all these things combined, for the first time in my life—and this has been true for many years now—I am creatively fulfilled and loving what I do: teaching and helping people around the world, even as I teach and help myself.

With hindsight, becoming aware of *how* I navigated the troubled waters of my life into my third and most rewarding career was a bonus offered by my "fear to fortune" story, and I'm humbled that I can share what I learned with you and others so that you might harness life's magic as I did.

Leveraging comprises seven very simple steps, each of which are fully laid out per chapter.

1. **Understand Your Power**: Not understanding the nature of our reality, and hence our power and its source, is the *number one* reason people actually "fail." With understanding, doubt is banished, confidence soars, and living deliberately becomes automatic.

2. **Chart Your Course**: Taking stock of where you now are, no matter where you are, and answering three simple

questions will reveal what you can immediately begin doing to bring about major life changes—even if you don't yet know exactly what you want.

3. **Take Action and Delegate**: Knowing what you can, should, and must do—versus what you mustn't ever do, what you must delegate—is crucial in leveraging the Universe and engaging life's magic.

4. **Leverage the Universe**: Beyond having a vision and physically moving with it, learning how to playfully use your thoughts, words, and deeds will bring exponential returns on your effort.

5. **Align Your Beliefs**: There's no need to figure out what invisible beliefs now limit you; they *are* invisible, after all! Instead, simply know what you want your beliefs to be, align them with your dreams, and begin installing them.

6. **Engage the Magic**: Starting and persisting make possible the critical yet unpredictable evolution of events, circumstances, and ideas that will ultimately bring about your dream's manifestation.

7. **Adjust Your Sails**: Even though you're now under full sail and your journey is progressing, there will not likely be any trace of "land on the horizon." Here's how to assure you're on course, in spite of appearances.

Fellow life adventurer, I've learned that when you stay grounded in the truth of life's magnificence and your glorious, divine power, all things become easier. Even better, an upward spiral of success and happiness will begin to lift off, gathering momentum to the point of you truly being unstoppable on your journey of self-discovery, revelation, and love. And with this still before you, no matter how rocking your life has been so far, I have no doubt that the *best* is yet to come.

A NOTE FROM THE UNIVERSE

What do you give someone who already has it all, forever and ever?

*Did you just say, "How about the fleeting illusion they don't have it all,
to create a sense of adventure, to fill their days with drama,
and to impose upon them the almost unbearable lightness
of being that all angels feel when dancing in
time and space ... dude"?*

Or was that "dude" actually a "duh"?

Don't believe in the fleeting illusions, dude.
The Universe

*P.S. For all the hoopla, heaven can get pretty boring without sometimes
believing in have and have not, here and there, now and then,
shaken not stirred.*

1

STEP ONE:

UNDERSTAND YOUR POWER

The first step to understanding your power lies in comprehending its source—the Universe—your relationship to it, and its magic. Just as you have to understand your car or computer to use them, your parents and children to appreciate them, or your friends and partners to enjoy them, so must you grasp how and where you fit into the Universe to leverage its infinite magic.

"But seek first the kingdom of God ... and all these things shall be added unto you."

I'm starting this chapter with a biblical quote from Matthew 6:33, even though I'm not remotely religious. Still, I consider myself to be extremely spiritual. I believe in God, the Universe, or a higher power that loves us all and is alive within each of us. I believe that we are eternal beings who preceded, and exist beyond, the illusions of time, space, and matter. I believe all religions are man-made, and while no doubt born of good intent, most have become dogmatic and exclusionary of those who don't accept or embrace their tenets.

I do *not* believe we are born to be tested, judged, and sentenced. I do *not* believe we are here to worship God or selflessly sacrifice our lives for others, but rather to be led by our dreams, follow our hearts, and be happy (which, ironically, is the most effective way to help others). I believe that every man and woman is of good intent, that love is the glue holding reality together, and that through our thoughts and focus we decide what this love will bring into our lives.

Still, I believe that the Bible (like many holy books, modern songs, or even greeting cards) has within it some stunningly beautiful and empowering nuggets of truth, which is why I occasionally quote from it, like the Matthew quote. It's just that many of these nuggets have been misinterpreted, misunderstood, or even redacted by religious leaders on occasion, and these inaccuracies have often been innocently accepted by "believers" who know nothing of the earlier edits (and might not have been believers if they did). For instance, reincarnation was originally in the Bible, according to Dr. Brian Weiss in his mega-international bestselling book *Many Lives, Many Masters*: "There were indeed references to reincarnation in the Old and the New Testaments. In AD 325 Roman emperor Constantine the Great ... had deleted references to reincarnation ... [and such deletions where later confirmed by] ... by The Second Council of Constantinople, meeting in AD 553."[1]

> **I believe that every man and woman is of good intent, that love is the glue holding reality together, and that through our thoughts and focus we decide what this love will bring into our lives.**

This Matthew quote I shared with you is just one of those nuggets of truth that has become misunderstood. I was raised a

1. Brian Weiss, *Many Lives, Many Masters* (New York: Fireside, 1988), 35.

Catholic, and what this quote meant to me growing up (and I think this is true for many Christians) is to seek first to live a good, honorable, clean life, according to Christian views, and then when you die, you'll go to heaven, where all things (being valued less than your mere entrance) will be given to you. But the meaning I take from this today, I believe, is more on point to its originally intended meaning, and far more beautiful. To me, it means to seek first to understand your true nature as a divine child of the Universe, worthy of all you can dream of having, blessed with love and power beyond comprehension, and then from such a lofty perspective, *finally understanding your true power and its source*, all things will be added unto you, here and now. Or, more simply, first grasp that you live in a world of illusions that are of your own creation, and then you can change those illusions to your liking.

This power over our illusions stems from the fact that our thoughts literally, eventually, and unfailingly become the things and events of our lives. *Thoughts become things* is the be-all and end-all principle of living the life of your dreams, of deliberately charting your course through the jungles of time and space. This is, as I mentioned in *Infinite Possibilities*, a pillar of this physical reality, *an absolute*, one of the Truths of Being that literally gives us a stage upon which to play out our lives. Since this is such a fundamental concept, let's briefly review the Truths of Being (from chapter 2 of *Infinite Possibilities*, "Beliefs"):

The Truths of Being: Life's Absolutes

We are all One (of One, of God, divine, interconnected). Nothing can exist outside of God or be "non-God." To be non-God, where would it come from? *What would it be made of?*

Thoughts become things (We are creators). Literally, our thoughts, *being pure God* for the prior truth, have an energy and a "life force" all their own.

Life is eternal (God, consciousness, energy, us). We are the creators of this illusory dimension of time (Einstein himself called it relative) so we must exist "before" it, and we will exist "after" it.

There is only Love (There is only God). Similar to, if not the same as, the first truth, this phraseology allows us to introduce the concept of love. Mustn't some form of love—divine love, undoubtedly far beyond what we practice as human love—be the motivation and reason behind *all* reality? Furthermore, could there possibly exist even a tiny forgotten pocket in reality that was forgotten, tainted, or miscreated into anything that wasn't full of divine love?

It's all good (Everything is exactly as it should be). This absolute allows for another concept to be addressed: "chance." In Divine Mind, even while all things remain possible, with infinite possibilities for expansion into unimaginable realms, in the deepest sense, ultimate outcomes, such as growing, learning, and remaining One with Divine Mind after the adventure, were *not* left to chance. There's no possibility for mistake, accident, *should have*, *maybe*, or *hope so* because the *general* potential for development was seen and understood at a higher level before our adventure began.

This list is not meant to be all-inclusive, as each of these truths could have a number of spin-offs, such as those offered in the parentheses, but the list is sufficient to obtain a solid grasp on the nature of our reality and to begin applying our power to fantastic effect. I'd also like to point out that of these truths, only one has a moving part, a variable: Thoughts Become Things. *And look who's thinking now!*

Beliefs versus the Truths of Being

These truths are absolute; they are immutable. They exist *even in the absence of belief in them,* creating the stage we live our lives upon. Now, that's big—really big!

The fact that you're open to reading a book like this tells me you already understand that beliefs are almighty. They are the fountainhead of all our thoughts, and those thoughts then go out and become the things and events of our lives. Yet even though our beliefs are that powerful, *thoughts become things* exists independently of beliefs. This principle comes first! *Meaning that even if you don't believe in this principle of* thoughts become things, *your thoughts will still become the things and events of your life!*

Religions have their truths, their pillars, but they are like movable feasts. One religion might say "he" is your savior; or "this" is the path; or "that" is the goal, while another religion will move the "legs of the table around," yet still promise salvation to its practitioners and to no one else. The principle of *thoughts become things,* like the other Truths of Being I've outlined, is not movable. It is not exclusionary. It makes no difference what your faith is or is not; your thoughts will always, unfailingly, create your experience.

A Note from the Universe

One of the coolest things about time and space is that it's impossible to kid oneself indefinitely.

Pow!
The Universe

Where You Fit in the Equation of Reality Creation

An odd thing happened in the years that followed my first realization that there had to be pillars to our reality and naming them, as I have above. I saw the obvious redundancy within them and began to think they could or should be collapsed into fewer truths. So I began to think that there might only be three immovable pillars, into which all the others seemed to fit:

There's only God.
We're all one.
Thoughts become things.

I was pretty proud of this idea and happy to have made my theory even simpler, but there was still a problem. Do you see there's still redundancy? If there's only God and we're all one, then aren't these the same thing?

So it dawned on me that perhaps there are only two Truths of Being. *There's only God* (or, we're all one—same thing) and *thoughts become things*. And while cautious, I was quite pleased with this, until I stepped back and pondered some more and once again saw the redundancy. If there's only God, what are *thoughts*—but God? And if there's only God, what are *things*—but God?

This led me to conclude that we could say there is really only one *Truth of Being*, one pillar to this reality that is absolutely immovable, and though you can say it many ways, the one I prefer is *thoughts become things*. This is the only terminology that immediately allows you to see where you fit into the equation of reality creation—as a thinker. I say "*a* thinker" so as not to offend and because God is unquestionably more than who we are (or better yet, God is unquestionably more than the extremely limited views we have of ourselves); but remember, *there's only God*, which means that saying "You are *the* Thinker" works just as well.

Given what's just been shared, here's an analogy that may help illustrate your role as a creator and just how you do what you do. You know of the comic book or have seen the movie *Spider-Man*, right? He shoots webs from the palm of his hands and navigates up and down Manhattan by swinging from skyscrapers. It dawned on me one day while thinking of the material for this book that we're all rather like Spider-Man, except instead of whipping out cobwebs, we whip out our thoughts as we focus them into time and space, which according to the distilled *Truths* is the same as saying we whip out God into time and space.

Whenever we think or focus, we're not conjuring up sterile, lifeless thoughts; *we're whipping out God into the world around us.* That's why this principle of *thoughts become things* is so powerful, and that's why we're so responsible for the things we choose to mentally dwell upon. When you focus your thoughts (your attention) in a certain direction, you are commanding God—your thoughts—into this realm of space, and in this realm of space, it is the law that your thoughts become the things and events of your life.

This way of looking at thoughts becoming things shows the immense power not only of thought *but of your own thoughts*, given your total freedom to choose the ones you'll entertain! You are sending God when you think of another person. You're sending God when you think of wealth and abundance. You're sending God when you think of poverty, lack, or unhappiness.

And on the plane of manifestation—where we effectively live—God, or this principle, will eventually reflect back to you *materially* the thoughts you've sent out. Fortunately, for any negativity we may inadvertently choose (and I think it's fair to say we all partake of this from time to time), most manifestations are *not* instantaneous. Furthermore, most negative thoughts are offset by our inherent optimism (we are usually *far* more optimistic than we realize) and our inborn inclination to prosper and thrive (more on this and negativity will be shared later). We are therefore naturally and instinctively, on the whole, more likely to experience "good" than "bad." Isn't your life already proof of this?

God versus the Universe

I realize I'm not using the term "God" here in any conventional sense, but rather as defined by the Truth of Being that *everything is God*. And by this definition, God includes your chosen focus and thoughts.

I think what most people want, however, is to believe in a God that has a personality—and not just any personality but one that is similar to their own. But while thinking that God has a personality offers a simplistic and manageable view of the Creator, it also implies that the Creator might also be judgmental, which negates the simple and otherwise obvious Truths of Being already laid out—in particular, the truth that *There is only Love*.

Of course I believe in "God," and of course I believe "It" must have some kind of faculty for *unconditional love*, far exceeding in beauty and support the type of love expressed by humans, but I'm very comfortable with the parallel realization that there is no such God as the one most of us were raised to believe in. And while I certainly can't wrap my head around the entirety of what God is, I can, like you, at least observe what *is* and what *feels right* and act accordingly, without having to think of God as a man or a woman, happy or angry, demanding or judgmental. This is what my Truths of Being attempt to do, name the obvious, and I hope it's evident that each of the truths empowers and celebrates all people, while excluding no one. Moreover, these truths give us, through thoughts becoming things, a foothold on *explaining* and using our inherent, self-evident supernatural powers.

While explaining what God is, to the degree possible and evident, I'd like to share a *Note from the Universe* I've referred to countless times while speaking in response to questions from audience members who ask, "So what is the Universe? Is it God? Can we count on it? Is it caring for us?"

A Note from the Universe

I know that you know that there's more to you than flesh and bone.

I know that you know that you're more than what time and space show.

And I know that you know that there's a greater self,
a greater you out there, beyond time and space, whether you call it
your guardian angel, your soul, or your greater self.

Yet I also know there's still some question in your mind as to who, what,
and where that other part of you is.

Well, I think the time has come to make the introduction.

Mike Dooley

It's me!

As you were,
The Universe

P.S. You weren't expecting some little Tinker Bell, were you?

The entire Universe is the other part of you. *This is where your power comes from.* And truly, the other part of you is so much more than a little pixie looking out for your best interests—or even a team of angels. Your family, friends, and neighbors are the other part of you. People going to work right now in China are the other part of you. I, Mike Dooley, am the other part of you. There is *nothing* that is not you. This is how connected we are; it's how we are all one. This is how powerful you are. You do not have a limit. That's how big you are. You are the eyes and the ears of the Universe in this incarnation of time and space, going by the name of whatever you go by, peering out at the world with your one-of-a-kind personality and perspectives, adding to the totality of what God is, *because you are pure God*!

You are the Universe. And your power comes from your ability to choose your all-powerful thoughts and send them out in any direction you decide upon. The only requirement, *if* you wish to live deliberately, is learning how to maintain your focus on what you want—in spite of any undesirable existing manifestations that have presented themselves according to earlier thoughts that you entertained before understanding this concept.

You are the Universe. And your power comes from your ability to choose your all-powerful thoughts and send them out in any direction you decide upon.

Thoughts Become Things

Thoughts become things fully explains how we have indeed been given dominion over all things. It's not a "sometimes" principle; it's an "all-the-time" principle. It doesn't work with just our positive thoughts; it works with all our thoughts. It's an immutable law that none of us can ever turn off, and it's as predictable and dependable as gravity. Of course, this isn't bad news. It's awesome news! Because we get to choose exactly what we're going to think, every minute of every day. With this principle, we can bring virtually anything we can imagine into our lives. And we're not just limited to acquiring material things; we can imagine more love, more joy, and more laughter.

Best of all, not one of us has to learn how to make our *thoughts become things* to use the principle any more than we have to learn how gravity works to be held by it. Our simple awareness is enough to begin slightly adjusting our life approaches in ways that will complement and deliberately harness nature's universal forces. This is what I'm offering you, and it begins with step one: understanding your power.

✻ TIME OUT ✻

To head off the rather obvious potential for criticism, the kind that was leveled at *The Secret* for the same reason: Do you think what I just shared about your thoughts becoming things is meant to imply that you can daydream your life better? That my message is one of visualizing day in and day out on your couch at home, perhaps with a vision board, and waiting for Oprah to call?

Also implicit in all my works is that taking action is a vital and mandatory part of facilitating change, which will be made abundantly clear in the chapters that follow. At a minimum, however, I'd like to think that readers automatically realize they should at least continue living their lives, out and about in the world, as they integrate what I'm sharing into their established routines. Better yet, based on tips that will follow in this book, I trust they'll take even more action. Yet for now, in chapter one, I'm simply explaining the basic tenets of our shared reality, and the point I'm making is that the entire physical world around us is made up of thought—our thoughts, your thoughts. We live in a hologram-like world of illusions that we project into place in ways far beyond our awareness, in keeping with some kind of grid or energy matrix that ensures consistency and continuity, both of which are pretty handy as they make possible the sharing of this "playing field," with geographic points of reference, physical laws, and undoubtedly much more.

While *how* we form our projections in time and space remains as unimportant to us as it is in our nighttime dreams, by at least recognizing that we must be creating our world of illusions through thought, we finally have an inroad into how we might deliberately create change—by first changing our thoughts. And while, again, rather obviously, the physical world will not instantaneously respond, our prior successes (in which we can readily see how our thoughts affected our lives) evidence, sure enough, that such changes in our thoughts do indeed influence how the rest of our lives will unfold.

Understanding this—your power—is the starting point for manifesting change.

✱ ✱ ✱

Thoughts become things. If you are alone, go to this principle. If you are broke, go to this principle. If you need answers, inspiration, ideas, or creativity, go to this principle. It is your salvation—*truly* the Holy Grail. It doesn't do you any good to pray in question marks. There is not a God "out there" to hear you. Your life is about you and your projections (the God that you "whip out" or project into the space of your life). To spark any kind of change you wish for, first go within.

It doesn't do you any good to pray in question marks.

It's as if our thoughts rearrange the sun, the moon, and the stars as they strive to become the things and events of our lives. Mountains are moved. Friends are summoned. Resources are tapped. Ideas are instilled. Inspiration, motivation, and courage are provided. And it works with the greatest of ease when we finally understand that our *thoughts become things* of their own volition, which will be made clearer as the book unfolds, and when we finally stop trying to manage every nuance of our progress from the extremely limited perspective of our physical senses alone. This latter approach is what I call "messing with the *cursed hows*," more commonly referred to by others, though they know not exactly why, as the "original sin."

The *Cursed Hows*

The original sin, as I see it, is committed whenever we base our behavior on the physical world around us *as if it were bedrock reality*! Typically we do this by using our physical senses to draw conclusions about ourselves, other people, the world and how it works, and, by extension, how we can successfully create change, even though this means being completely oblivious to the deeper spiritual dimension from which the physical world as we know it originates—our thoughts.

Adam and Eve

As the well-known story of Adam and Eve goes, they were the first two humans, who fell from grace by biting into the apple of knowledge and for doing so, they were then expelled from the Garden of Eden. I propose that this story is actually a metaphor for two spiritual beings (as we all are) living in the captivating *yet entirely illusionary* jungles of time and space. The apple was tempting, of course, because it seemed so real, *even though they knew better* (this awareness being symbolized by God warning them not to eat the apple).

Biting into the apple was tantamount to *buying into knowledge*, giving the world revealed by their physical senses precedence over the world revealed by their inner senses. This act signified a tipping point from which they no longer perceived the world around them as illusionary but as real. After all, who would bite into an illusion? From then on, their behavior would be guided by the illusions of time and space, as perceived by their physical senses. The entire story of the Fall is about *our* forgetting the truth concerning the very essence of what is real, and thus forgetting how to navigate our lives through time and space. Hence the expression "the truth shall set you free," as in, free from illusions and back to your mastery over them *as you rediscover your power and oneness with God*.

No problem, though. You might even say it was part of "the plan." Besides, we're eternal, so we'll get it straightened out. In the meantime, the great boon to believing in these illusions—all of them—is that they actually *make possible* our adventures in time and space. The price we pay, however, for recommitting this original sin every day (believing that the illusions are more real than the Spirit and thoughts that give rise to them) is that we become "stuck" in these illusions. Instead of waking up to the truth that we are creating them, we react to them and thereby perpetuate them (sometimes creating a hell for ourselves as a result of the sense of powerlessness that inevitably ensues), as our thoughts become the things and events of our lives!

The *cursed hows* I speak of arise when we primarily use our physical senses to draw conclusions about *how* our dreams and desires will come to pass, when in reality all manifestations are born of thought and far more is involved, logistically speaking, for any dream to come true than we could ever comprehend with our tiny brains. And because we can sense our mortal inability to intentionally plot and insist upon physical progress, we can become overwhelmed, anxious, and get totally psyched out! But when we understand the truth behind all manifestations, we can start initiating change from the inside out, beginning with a vision and then physically showing up to be availed of life's magic, leaving the actual *hows* to divine intelligence.

A NOTE FROM THE UNIVERSE

True, while there really is no such thing as "judgment," "wrong," or "sin," as you've likely been taught, there remain such things as consequences.

And can you imagine the consequences of misunderstanding that "all are one," "there's only love," and "thoughts become things"? Phew!

I really did try to think of everything.
The Universe

P.S. Of course, in the long run, these consequences clear up such misunderstandings pretty handily.

The Truth about Hell

When you mess with the *cursed hows*, two horrendous things happen. Number one, you carry the weight of the world on your shoulders, thinking you, and you alone, must micromanage the journey that will make your dreams come true. With such an approach, life's magic simply isn't able to reach you through "chance" events and encounters, as you leave no room for it when you insist on certain outcomes and specific circumstances that are supposed to unfold on your terms. Every disappointment feels like a major setback. Frustration is at every turn. Sometimes the journey can become one in which you feel pitted *against* your dream instead of aligned with it. It becomes the enemy, the cause of your discomfort and depression, and you feel utterly powerless before it.

The second horrendous thing that happens when you mess with the *cursed hows* is that you *limit* an otherwise unlimited Universe. You tie Its hands, even though It always knows the fastest, shortest, most harmonious path to your heart's desire. If you knew this, you'd have faith and let it work things out for you (as you continue to otherwise take action, which is covered in chapter 2 and beyond). But because this is not how we've been taught life works, we don't have faith, and without it, we must sweat the details and mess with the *cursed hows*!

When *Cursed Hows* Become *Cursed Whos*

Wanting a *certain someone* to be in our life, often to the point that it breaks our heart, is a perfectly common example of messing with the *cursed hows*—using our physical senses to assess only a glimmering of the world around us and drawing conclusions as if we could physically see all our options.

How many people do you know really well? Ten? Fifty? One hundred? Two hundred? Now, how many does your greater self, the Universe, know? So wouldn't it make sense to let the Universe pick your ideal partner from billions, as opposed to tens or hundreds? In choosing the person who's right for you, don't rely solely upon your limited assessment of reality. If you turn the equation of having a great partner over to the Universe, the odds that this person might be from your relatively small inner circle are still included, but you also become available to someone you haven't met yet.

That is, until you begin insisting that your soul mate will come from your inner circle: "Oh, dear Universe, let it be Mary, my soul mate! Mary completes me. Please let Mary love me as much as I love her!" But what if the ideal person for you is Sarah, whom you've yet to meet? Because of your insistence on Mary, from your limited view of your immediate options, Sarah is no longer an option! You close yourself down and shut yourself out from the opportunity to meet Sarah by insisting on the *how* (or in this case, the *who*) of your dream to have Mary as your partner. You have turned the equation of having a great partner into one that exclusively includes Mary. Yet it's not about Mary; it's about you and your ideal partner. Let me assure you that once you finally loosen up on the reins a bit and finally meet your "Sarah," whoever it is, you won't care so much about your "Mary." "Hey, Sarah. Look over there, in the food court! I know that girl from work, Mary. I used to like her—not like I like *you*, but she was nice. Gee, I hope she finds someone!"

When *Cursed Hows* Don't Make "Cents"

We've been raised in a spiritually primitive society that has erroneously taught us that to create change in our lives, we must first

17

figure out how we're going to do it! This can also severely limit us when we dream of living in wealth and abundance. We wonder, "How am *I* going to make *that* happen?" We can visualize living in financial splendor all day long, but when our feet hit the ground, we tend to panic! Then we come up with ideas like, "I know! I'll write a book! Oprah will interview me! And the world will beat a path to my door!" A few days later, remembering that even writing to-do lists can overtax us, we become despondent, overwhelmed, and disgusted with ourselves!

What really happens when we mess with the *cursed hows* is that we unwittingly rewire our brains, creating beliefs and expectations without knowing it. And then you've saddled the dream of writing a book, or whatever, with creating your wealth and abundance, which is obviously quite a problem for the nonwriter! Just think how stymied your creativity might become when you *think* it's your one and only ticket to wealth and abundance.

I've been down that road myself far too many times. I've learned very simply that if you want to write a book, invent a gadget, or start a company, do it because you *love* everything about the thought of it, not because it's going to be *how* some other dream of yours will come to pass. The Universe knows countless ways your dreams can be realized. Yet to use your physical senses and logically say, "This is how," is like slamming the door on all of them. You'll completely stress yourself out while limiting an otherwise unlimited Universe.

A NOTE FROM THE UNIVERSE

Do you have any idea how many princesses have gone unrecognized by their prince because of logic? Or how many princes have gone unrecognized by their princess because of pride?

How many dreams were dashed when the handmaiden answered the door? Or when the gatehouse was mistaken for the mansion? Or when the calm before the storm of abundance and good fortune was viewed as a sign to retreat?

Happily, we've got forever and ever. And fortunately, it's never too late to see what one's missed, remain focused on the dream instead of the hows, and move with unwavering faith.

Yeeeeeee-haaaaaaaaaa!
The Universe

P.S. Oh no, don't feel sorry for the handmaiden! She stuck around, her prince showed up, they inherited the mansion, and they were showered in good fortune forever and ever.

All You Need to Know

Your *thoughts become things*. They always have, and they always will. This is your divine inheritance. This is how you can change your life. It's *the* answer. It's the solution. It's *the* salvation of all who discover it. As I said at the beginning of this chapter, it reveals where you fit into the equation of reality creation: and that is as a creator yourself. *You* create your corner of the world and all that you experience.

So for me, years ago, while I could not explain how the train of my life had seemingly fallen off its tracks, I could nevertheless explain the basic tenets of this reality. I knew how things worked, generally speaking, and that *I* would have to work with them if I wanted change. And knowing that my thoughts became the things and events of my life, I realized that if I was going to get this party started again, it wouldn't do me any good to beseech some unknown Universe outside of myself, asking for a lucky break, a miraculous turn of events, or a free ride. Changes in my life would have to come about from within myself. I knew that if I knuckled down and became vigilant with all I thought, said, and did, aligned my beliefs with the life of my dreams, and got started taking lots of action, then it would be enough to change everything. And so I began to chart my course, and you can too.

———————— Summary Points ————————

* Understanding the truth about how life works, our power, and its source not only sets you free, it creates the rock from which we can deliberately shape our lives.
* There is a God (the Universe, Divine Intelligence) of which we are made and one with; hence, we are part of that God, come alive within the dream of life.
* We are the creators of our every experience, and we create through our focus. One of life's absolutes is that our thoughts literally become the things and events of our lives.
* *Thoughts become things* fully explains how we have indeed been given dominion over all things.
* *How* our thoughts will become things and exactly how our dreams will come true is beyond our ability to calculate and know. Yet insisting on certain "hows" actually limits life's magic.
* The Universe—our "greater selves"—always knows the shortest, fastest, and most harmonious way that our dreams can come true.

———————— SUGGESTED EXERCISES ————————

Your Thoughts That Have Become Things

What have you been thinking? We don't often appreciate that many of our past thoughts have already become a reality in our present lives. Look around at your life today—the material possessions you've accumulated, the relationships you've built and nurtured, the experiences you've had, and the person you've become. What thoughts of yours have already come to pass with regard to:

* Work and career?
* Your relationships?
* Your home?
* Your social life?
* Your health and appearance?

In a journal or on blank paper, write out your answers and include thoughts on as many other areas of your life and experiences that you can think of.

Your Thoughts That Will Become Things

Where would you like to take your life now, and how will it look once you arrive? Use this exercise to create a vision(s) using words or pictures to help you imagine the life you want to live, without regard to *how* you will make it happen. Again, using a journal or blank paper, consider every area of your life you'd like to create change in, perhaps beginning with the places noted in the first exercise.

2

STEP TWO:

CHART YOUR COURSE

The second step in leveraging the Universe and engaging life's magic is to give ourselves direction by charting a course. Beyond the obvious need we all have for direction, charting a course is going to help you answer that age-old question that has bamboozled humans since the beginning of time: "What am I going to do when I grow up?" By the end of this chapter, you'll either know the answer for yourself or you'll be on your way to eventually uncovering it within weeks, if not days. This chapter presupposes that you don't yet know what you're one day going to be doing with your life, and therefore that you're likely drawing a complete blank with what you could now be doing to get there! If you feel you're already on your way, then this part of the book may help give you confirmation and some new ideas for speeding things up.

To make this as simple as possible, realize that when it comes to charting a course by starting where you are, you have only three questions to answer. And the best news is, even if you don't know the answer to all three (which you probably don't or you wouldn't be wondering what you might do when you "grow up"), you'll see that by beginning where you are and at least doing something—anything—the unanswered questions will eventually be answered for you. "Chart Your Course" might imply more work than is really necessary. This chapter is designed to simply *get you moving* by making the entire process far easier than you've ever let it be before. The three questions are:

1. What do I want? (Targeting your destination.)

2. Where am I today? (Establishing your starting point.)

3. Which paths will I take? (Charting your course.)

What Do I Want?

Many people wondering where they want to go with their life approach me with questions that sound a lot like this: "How do I find that special niche that only I can fill?" "How do I discover my purpose?" "How can I know what I should be doing with my life?" Yikes! Can you see how from the get-go the original question of "What do I *want?*" has very subtly turned into questions preloaded with assumptions—assumptions that render them unanswerable, assumptions that have nothing to do with what you really *want?*

In the first chapter, we talked about the nature of our reality and saw that you are a creator. You're now careening through eternity, rediscovering yourself, your playfulness, and your incredible, almost unbelievable powers. You're not here to save anybody! You're not here *to fill* some kind of career niche! You're not here to find out what the right job is for you!

You're here simply because you, a fragment of God, wanted to be here. You chose to be here to see what might happen, based on the choices you'd make once you arrived. You're here for the adventure of it. You're here to let your desires take you wherever they may. *You are here to be you!*

You're here simply because you, a fragment of God, wanted to be here.

You are precious and extraordinarily unique. Your existence as you were, are, and will become is a vital part of the whole. Your insights are irreplaceable; you see with your eyes a view of the world that has *never* been seen before. You hear with your ears what has *never* been heard before. You feel with your heart what has *never* been felt before. And with this gift of existence, all you have to do is simply be yourself.

Life—the whole thing—is a discovery process, an adventure process, a fun-and-games process. There are no preconditions. There are no prerequisites. You can have whatever you want. That means there are no *shoulds*! *Shoulds* imply limits and obligations. Or they imply that you're concerned about what other people think, fitting into some kind of mold, making enough money, or the like. There's nothing helpful or empowering about *shoulds*.

But notice what happens when we go back to the guiding, and long since forgotten, question that actually sparked the confusion most people are tangled with: "What do I *want?*" Returning to this, to your primal, divine *desire*, while pitching the *shoulds*, will completely reorient you as it recasts how you see the world around you and puts you in a clearer place for charting your course. In many instances, it will also bring you back into the present, rather than have you living in the future, since the question is primarily concerned with what you want *now*.

This step of asking what you want and getting to the root of things doesn't just apply to life-changing career choices; it applies to *everything*—even the simplest things. Too often we fall into the "should trap" because our society is of the notion that if we don't figure out the *shoulds* and *hows* ahead of time, we're being recklessly irresponsible. After all, no one is going to figure it out for us! Yet such thinking completely neglects the spiritual side of life, our divine heritage, and the magic we've always been free to tap into.

When the weekend comes, for instance, I often think to myself, "What *should* I do this weekend?" Or when it comes to writing a new book or another *Note from the Universe*, I'll think, "Hmm, what *should* I write?" It's another offshoot of the spiritually primitive times we live in that we often just think in terms of *shoulds*. And to compound the issue, not only do most people think that creating change in their lives must begin with physical effort, calculated entirely based on the world (the *illusion*) around them, but then we're labeled selfish if we're led by what we want instead of what is good for others, further causing us to think in terms of *shoulds*!

If I ask myself instead, "Do I *want* to work on a new book?" suddenly it's easy to answer. Or for the weekend, if I ask, "Do I *want* to go here or there?" Then that's easy too. "Who do I *want* to spend time with?" "What do I *want* to give priority to in my life?" These all become easy questions to answer.

Clarity is magnified when you change the word *should* to *want*, and this substitution becomes easier to allow yourself to do when you *understand* that whatever payoff the *should* would have theoretically provided—like comfort, safety, or even abundance— is dependent more upon the Universe and life's magic (once leveraged and engaged) than your choosing the right *should*. The Universe and life's magic are best engaged when you're happy, doing what you want.

If you need further convincing of life's magic working in all fields, consider that there's no career, profession, or endeavor to choose from that somebody else hasn't already chosen before you—and been wildly successful at. So dream big, follow your heart, do what you want, and let the magic unfold.

To offer a bit more clarity, and to perhaps shatter some preconceived *shoulds* you may still secretly harbor, here's another *Note from the Universe*—one of my all-time favorites:

A NOTE FROM THE UNIVERSE

Do you think I ultimately reward those who live in poverty?
Do you think those who toil and sweat from paycheck to paycheck are
more likely to inherit the Kingdom than those who work in ivory towers?
Do you think I take special notice of your sacrifices?
Am I pleased when you put the needs of others before your own?
Do you think I favor those who strive to live spiritual lives?

Actually, dearest, I don't give a flying yahoo.

I love you no matter what rules you make up.

Talk about unconditional,
The Universe

Now, while that *Note* may feel like a little slap to some, do you not see the *absolute* truth in it? The alternative is to believe that Divine Intelligence is not only judgmental but that It has favorites, which means God's love has *conditions*. It's funny to hear people talk about unconditional love, because it virtually never is. Beneath these sentiments are silent words: "So long as you love me, so long as you're reasonable and treat me with respect, so long as you love me as I love you, and so long as you don't hurt anyone," and so on. Sorry, but these are conditions: conditions that do not exist in terms of the Universe's love for us. It's that simple. You have that kind of backing. You are worthy, you do deserve whatever it is you want—and you can have it.

To get back on track and make headway into charting a course by starting where you are, the first of the three questions to ask yourself has to do with knowing what you want. Asking what you want is about being yourself and understanding that you are capable, worthy, and deserving of manifesting a life based on your own preferences.

❋ TIME OUT ❋

It's not just tangling with the forbidden fruit and logic that's kept us from considering what it is we most want, placing our desires behind our *shoulds*, but also the corrupt rationale that humankind is a beast of sorts, born of sin, driven by a mysterious subconscious mind, susceptible to evil, destined to wreak havoc! "We can't all just do whatever we want! That's irresponsible! Dangerous! Nothing would ever get accomplished!"

The real shock to me is that we have indeed, as a civilization, been as wildly successful as we have with global commerce, breathtaking technological breakthroughs, and mass cooperation between virtually all countries, in spite of the spiritual naïvetés that have kept us from following our bliss and living joyful lives, all achieved while shackled in lives of drudgery. The premise I live by, and that I see alive and well all over the world, is that human beings are kind, of good intent, instinctively giving, caring, and loving. We're not here by accident but by the design of an intelligence so profound that we cannot even imagine it, and the fastest way to find heaven on earth would be for all of us to actually place our desires before our *shoulds*, which rather than leading us to Armageddon would lead to a blossoming kindness, good intent, giving, caring, and loving, the likes of which this planet has never known.

There is enough for everyone on this illusionary planet where our *thoughts become things*. And our natural instincts would automatically ensure that we behave responsibly so as to guarantee that tomorrow does indeed come with all the same promises and potentials that today holds, rather than spoiled and polluted. The reason we see a very small portion of the world's people behaving, at times, so horribly, *as if* possessed by evil, is not the result of us following our passions but of our wholesale neglect of them and the tensions, resentment, and fear this has created.

❊　❊　❊

But What If You Don't Even Know What You Want?

Keeping this understanding in mind and by reframing our questions with our dreams, the entire game changes, and we have step one of three for charting a course under our belts—unless, of course, you are where I was not so long ago and you don't even know what you want! I, too, had spent most of my life messing with the *shoulds*, concerned with things that don't really matter and losing touch with what I actually wanted.

I remember watching the Biography Channel and seeing people featured who were living out their passions. I remember saying to Andy, "If I only knew what my passion was, *I'd do it*. I'd do it with gusto! I'd give it everything!" But I didn't know what I wanted to do as I faced starting my life over. If this is the case for you, what you want can literally be revealed to you, as will the course to chart—all of which is covered in the material ahead—once you begin *physically* doing what you can, with what you have, from where you are today.

Where you are in your life today is never *who* you are.

Where Am I Today?

This is the easiest of the three questions to answer, unless you make it unnecessarily hard and/or complicated, which I'll help you avoid.

For starters, I'll guess that today—and this is based on the presumption that started this chapter (that you don't yet know what you really *want*)—you now either:

1. *Are doing something you're not that wild about.*

2. *Have nothing to do, no life traction. "Your car is idling in park," whether of your choosing or not (you were laid off, had an accident, or other).*

So which is it? Answering 1 or 2 is all you need do in order to move on to the third question of which paths you might take, which will at last give you direction. But first we must free you from the past and help you keep this simple.

Where you are in your life today is never *who* you are. Moreover, you needn't explain or justify where you are in order to move forward. Another unfortunate condition imposed upon us by our primitive times is the notion that we must both explain and justify where we are so that we can learn from our mistakes and logically move on (for example, chart a course). Rubbish.

I'm all for learning from mistakes, but let's first be certain we've even made some before we jump to the conclusion that we're somehow flawed because of our immediate circumstances. I'll share more in chapter 5, "Align Your Beliefs," which will help convince you of this, but the gist of what you'll learn there is that just because you don't yet have what you want, or even if it seems like you've taken two steps back when you thought you'd be moving forward, does not mean that there's something wrong with you or your course.

Your current situation of not yet having what you want may simply be a matter of deeper priorities of yours that haven't been acknowledged but are still of importance to you, or it may be that the fastest way to get to where you want to go actually involves a detour "for your own good." Yet as soon as you begin thinking or claiming that something is wrong with you, you immediately buy into issues that will quickly become yours, even though they had *nothing* to do with whatever setbacks you seemingly encountered!

Another problem with the approach of "explaining and justifying" your situation stems from the rationale that with an intellectual analysis of our situation, we'll be better able to logically move on. Oh no! The apple of knowledge again! There goes any hope for integrating your new spiritual awareness into the fresh steps you'll be taking, because now you're going to be sweating the *cursed hows*—in other words, worrying about exactly how your dream will come true, trying to be in the right place at the right time, with the right thing to say to the right person, because, after all, opportunity only knocks once. Sheesh!

And, of course, this purely logical approach never even takes into consideration whether or not it (the logical approach) is what got you into the pickle you may now be in (although, as I said a few paragraphs ago, it's even better not to assume you're in a pickle). All you need to do is know where you're starting from:

1. *Are you doing something you're not that wild about?*

2. *Do you now have nothing to do, no life traction?*

Which Paths Will I Take?

Whatever your answer to question 2 above, the next question becomes, "Which paths will I now take?" Keeping with the premise of this chapter, this question again assumes you don't yet know what you want to do; otherwise, you'd be doing it with gusto! Yet if you aren't sure what you'll one day be doing, how can you choose the right path? This might seem to make charting a course next to impossible, but as I've said, you don't have to know the answers to all these questions, *or even the first two*, in order for there to eventually be illumination.

A NOTE FROM THE UNIVERSE

When just starting out on a new journey, it's only natural to feel
vulnerable. After all, it may seem that you have much to lose. But may I
remind you that never again, at any other point in your journey,
will you have so much to gain as you will if you start today?

I'll take that as a yes.

Tallyho!
The Universe

You're Doing Something You're Not That Wild About

If this describes you, and you don't yet know what it is you want to be doing, my advice, which may seem abrasive at first, is really very simple: keep doing what you're doing, *but do it better*. If you're looking and looking, your gaze always locked on the horizon for something better, you're probably not giving your all to where you now are. You're not fully present. In fact, the more you dislike whatever you're doing, the worse you're probably doing it. Yet if you don't master what's in front of you, it will (if it hasn't already) master *you*.

I saw this play itself out when I worked at Price Waterhouse (PW, before the Coopers & Lybrand merger). When people are hired for entry-level positions in the big accounting firms, generally straight out of college, they almost all hate their jobs. It's the first time in their lives that they have to be somewhere five, sometimes even six or seven days a week, at the crack of dawn, working long hours. They lose the option of sleeping in, staying up late, and doing those other fun things they probably did before their work lives began. Yuck! Yet the policy at PW was, and I imagine still is, if you're not *promoted* within three years, you're let go. In other words, if you don't master what's in front of you, you're fired.

But let me clarify. When I say, "Master what's in front of you," I'm not talking about becoming the gold medalist or the best in the world. I mean doing *your* best—your best with what you've got, from where you are. Attitude plays a huge role here—appreciating that you have something to do, seeing it as a stepping-stone to something better, and making the best of your situation with a smile and a glad heart. That's mastering what's in front of you. That's giving it your full attention. At these firms, when you're promoted, guess what: that old job that you hated *is gone!* You're suddenly free of it! Now you have a new job title. You have new responsibilities, maybe even subordinates. Sometimes even options for specializing present themselves, and suddenly the scenery radically changes, whereas those people who didn't master what's in front of them are forced into finding something else to do, for someone else, probably back at the bottom rung of another company, still hating what they do.

Within the following three years at PW, the same thing happened: you were either promoted or released. And this continued until, typically twelve years with the firm, you either become a partner or it's adios! In life, the promotions might not be vertical; they might be horizontal or tangential, one leading to another. But the same idea applies. Over time, you gain a higher—and usually improved—view of the world around you. You get to know who people are. People get to know who you are. And your choices for specializing, generalizing, or completely "changing horses" (by working for yourself or a client) start multiplying.

Remember that the other part of you is the Universe and, by extension, the other part of everyone else is the Universe. We *are* one. If you hate your job or if you're uncommitted, people sense it. On the other hand, if you love your job or are at least doing your best, people sense this too. Those who are doing their best, mastering what's before them to the degree they can, are the same people who are given new opportunities. Life then eventually lifts them *free of the job they didn't like.* This is the Universe in action, or, better, reacting to our actions, adding to our momentum, multiplying our efforts.

People fear that if they do their unpleasant job better and apply themselves to it more, it may give cause for their employers to *leave them* where they are—that an excellent performance of "cleaning the toilets" will keep them in that position for life! Yet how many employers aren't ultimately (and deeply) interested in the bottom line? How many employers, therefore, would let their most talented people stay at the bottom? How many aren't *always* on the lookout for ways to delegate more responsibilities to able hands? In life, as soon as you master what's in front of you, you're raised to the next level and choices abound, whereas if you don't master what's in front of you, life will let you flounder.

Of course, all my references in this chapter have been to your career, because that's where we spend most of the hours of our life (whether you work for pay, volunteer, or raise a family) and because this is where I see people wanting the most help for expanding their life. But this system of "being your best" and raising your life to new heights is evident in every level of our existence.

In life, as soon as you master what's in front of you,
you're raised to the next level and choices abound,
whereas if you don't master what's in front of you,
life will let you flounder.

Consider relationships. People who care, to the degree of taking action and putting themselves out into the world, looking their best, doing their best for others, giving, sharing, and following their heart, are literal magnets for friends and partners. Everybody wants "some of what they have." Good cheer is always contagious.

Or consider health. Those who do their best with what they have, who eat, exercise, rest, play, and work well, are generally in better health than ones who don't. Or how about abundance? People who care about abundance and go out into the world with abundance creation on their mind (rather than simply visualizing it and making no attempts to physically avail themselves of it) will eventually be in a place where they create and possess abundance. (It's beyond their control—they couldn't stop it if they wanted to.)

Of course, you can point to exceptions within these generalities I've just shared, *but they would be exceptions*, hardly "proof" that the Universe and life's magic don't respond to our attitudes and behaviors. And for the ambitious student who'd like to understand these exceptions better, I invite you to consider my lengthy explanations in both *Infinite Possibilities* and *Manifesting Change* for why some of our thoughts do not become things and why some things happen that we have never thought about in advance—to the point of being born into famine in a third-world country (or in the United States). For this book, however, more than ample evidence exists in all our lives that when we master what is before us, the Universe magically responds.

A NOTE FROM THE UNIVERSE

Treating "any old job" as if it were your dream job is the fastest way to spark the kind of life changes that will yield your dream job.

Same for any old house, friend, day, life—or pair of espadrilles.

Yeah,
The Universe

Suddenly, Clarity

Once you master what's in front of you, one of two things will happen: One, through the promotions that life gives you over time, you'll see clearly on the horizon exactly what it is that you'd most like to be doing. Or, two, which is actually how it worked for me and will far more likely be how it works for you, through life's "promotions" and the countless subtle changes that will begin permeating your life, you'll wake up one morning with a different job, different responsibilities, and surrounded by different people, and you'll be amazed to find that you're *already* living the life of your dreams. It works like this because as you become absorbed with mastering what's in front of you, doing it better, appreciating that you have something, and making the best of your situation (which does *not* imply you will ever "settle for less"), your life will ease, almost imperceptibly, into an entirely new realm.

You'll then ask the question, the same that I ask to this very day, "How did this happen to *me*? This is *even better* than my wildest dreams. What did I ever do to deserve so much?" Or, as asked by Khalil Gibran's beloved character Almustafa in *The Prophet*, "If this is my day of harvest, in what fields have I sowed the seed, and in what unremembered seasons?"

When you keep busy, doing even better work and becoming an even better person, miracles happen. You probably won't recognize them as miracles, but small adjustments in your life begin occurring. This is how our *thoughts become things*: they first become circumstances. It's as if our thoughts go out into the world, rearranging people and events like puppets on marionette strings—you being the unknowing puppeteer—so that you will be predisposed to life's so-called coincidences, happy accidents, and serendipities. *As you're taking action*, connections will be made in the unseen epiphanies received and inspiration instilled, yet only in hindsight will you be able to look back at the trail you've tread to see where the miracles occurred. (I'll review this in chapter 6.)

You Now Have Pretty Much Nothing to Do

If you currently have pretty much nothing to do and don't yet know what you want to do, my advice, which this time may seem naïve, is also really simple: *Do anything!* Give yourself a deadline, like two weeks or even two days, to take some type of action or baby steps in a certain direction, volunteering, visiting employment agencies, or networking with new people and/or groups. Just go do it! The only mistake you can make is *not* doing something.

My experience with audiences is that there can be resistance to this, which usually sounds something like this: "I can't go out and do anything! If I just go out and get some job at the mall, what if Oprah calls and I'm not home? What if my ship comes in and I'm not there for it?" Because they don't know what they want to do or even *should* do, it's no wonder they end up paralyzed into doing nothing, waiting on the sidelines of life for a miracle.

There's only one place the ship of your dreams will never find you, and that's sitting at home waiting for it. If all you're doing to create change in your life is waiting for the phone to ring, Oprah won't be calling, nor will Prince (or Princess) Charming be showing up at your door anytime soon.

On the other hand, no matter what path you take, simply by being out in the world, metaphorically stirring up the magic, you'll have engaged the Universe. Contact! You'll then be available for those coincidences and serendipities that will guide you to the right place at the right time, and your ship *will* find you. It always does. Going out into the world consistently, no matter the direction or what you do, is the first step to triggering two things that will then aid you in finding direction and charting your course to discovering your preferences and getting feedback and confirmation from life.

Discovering Your Preferences

First, you'll realize that you have preferences. You'll realize that you're not as lost as you'd thought you were, that you do in fact have things that you want to do. They might not be or seem like your "dream come true," but preferences will arise. Giving yourself a deadline for taking action is key because then you'll quickly start ruling out all the other things that you positively don't want to do! From there, you'll be able to narrow your options to a few things that you'd prefer doing. At least then you're on the move. I realize these choices you choose from may only be the least unattractive of all the other unattractive options before you! Nevertheless, they're going to give you a direction to move in. Even if it means taking a job that you're not thrilled about, if it's the least unattractive of your unattractive options, take it and do it well.

This is not about choosing a new life career; this is about starting something that will eventually lead to a new career, one that will reveal itself in time. This is not about finding your true love but availing yourself of that possibility. All you have to do is start knocking on doors within two weeks or, better yet, two days, asking questions, turning over stones, searching and exploring. Do you see how this works? You can immediately start making changes, having a direction, and moving down a path—within days.

Receiving Feedback and Confirmation from Life

The second thing to happen, which can only occur once you've started on a path, is that life will start talking to you; the Universe will start giving you a thumbs-up or a thumbs-down.

This is what happened to me all those years ago. I didn't know what I was going to do with my life, but I knew that I had to do something. Looking at my options, I was able to narrow them down to two *palatable* choices. I say "palatable" because that's all they were. These were not dream choices, but they were the beginnings of an outline for charting my course, steps that would at least give me something to do. So I looked at my options. Number one, I was still a licensed Certified Public Accountant (CPA) in the state of Florida. Number two, I was still sending out the "Monday Morning Motivators," free emails from the defunct T-shirt company that offered inspiration to subscribers.

Rather than limit myself to one direction or the other, I decided to set out on both paths. So I created a résumé bragging about my PW experience and running my own company for ten years afterwards, and started circulating it on employment websites as I reviewed employment ads in the *Orlando Sentinel*, *Miami Herald*, and *New York Times*. I was pretty sure that somebody would snap me up in no time at all!

After about six weeks of pounding the pavement, with every step I took, I realized that my heart wasn't in it. I submitted each application with dread, thinking of what it would be like to go back into accounting or the corporate world. Yet to my *utter dismay*, nobody would even give me an interview! It then occurred to me that as an entrepreneur who ran my own company for ten years, and with that company no longer in business, perhaps I wasn't such a "hot commodity" after all. This added up to a double confirmation: my heart wasn't in it *and* no one wanted me. In other words, having at least knocked on the door of the corporate world, I discovered something that I hadn't known before: that not moving further on this path was win-win for me—and future employers!

Subsequently, something else happened that helped me become even clearer about the direction I'd be moving in. The treasurer of a huge Orlando-based global company asked me to meet with him. It was a "sympathy interview" from a friend of my neighbor, who was that company's CEO. After hearing my story the treasurer looked me straight in the eye and said, "Mike, what are you doing here? You've got what I've always wanted. You've got what everybody here has always wanted—your own company." A bit shocked, I wanted to protest. I wanted to say, "But . . . you don't understand. We've liquidated everything. There are no more products. No more customers. Nothing." Surely he'd misunderstood.

But he hadn't missed a thing. There was something in his words that rang like bells in my heart. The more I thought about what he said, and the more I reassessed my situation, the more I realized there may still be work to do at tut.com. After all, even though only a shell of a company remained, it was still a legal enterprise. We had *not* gone out of business; we had merely stopped doing business. It still had a database of "fans" and potential shoppers. Plus, I calculated that I had an estimated two and a half years during which I could financially coast—the luxury of being able to take my time and not act out of desperation. Yes, confirmation!

At the same time, the "Monday Morning Motivators" came alive! Something amazing happened: I not only discovered the process of creative writing but found I also enjoyed it, something I had never even dreamed I might like. No longer was I bound by rhyming poems that had to fit onto T-shirts. These mailings consisted of a poem that had been previously written for a TUT T-shirt, followed by a new editorial on the theme of that poem. I wrote to the best of my ability, mastering what was before me, sending out this weekly inspirational message for free to a thousand or so people. And since I had the time, for every mailing sent, I spent hours crafting it (even though they were only two or three paragraphs long). I would take as long as necessary, until that inner feeling told me, "Yeah, that's good. *I* really like it."

I loved this process, which was a huge "aha" for me, a thumbs-up from the Universe, my greater self, that I was headed in a positive direction. When I got to the end of my two- or three-hour exercise, I was filled with a sense of creative fulfillment that I had never known before in my life. And then, to top things off, something else even more unexpected happened: people began replying and enthusiastically saying things like, "Wow, Mike, that was really great! I hope you're saving these for a book one day!" "Hey, Mike, I'm looking forward to Mondays now!" and "Mike, thanks for taking the time to write us."

Feeling good about what I was doing *and* receiving the positive feedback were "rewards," if you will, that I simply could not have anticipated until I took my first tentative baby steps in the direction of writing. After action comes clarity. Only after your first step can you begin to take your second. Do something— *do anything*!

> Only after your first step can you begin to take your second. Do something—*do anything*!

One Small Step Is Not Just One Small Step

As I've touched upon, one of the misperceptions I've observed is that people think if they take an hourly job, work for free, or do something that doesn't light up every cell in their body, they're settling for less. They begin rationalizing and thinking, "I know *thoughts become things.* I know I have dominion over all things. I know the Universe conspires on my behalf—so why should I do something beneath me?" They think that by doing something that's less than their dreamed-of result, they're compromising. So instead, they do nothing and wait for the Universe to come to their rescue.

There are better ways to view these first steps. What might seem to be small and insignificant progress may actually make possible later giant leaps that cannot even be anticipated now. What's more, it's precisely these small steps, as I have said many times already, that will avail you of life's magic, which cannot reach you otherwise.

A NOTE FROM THE UNIVERSE

The thing that most forget while dreamily looking off into the horizon for the ship of their dreams to come into port is that such ships never sail in but are actually built beneath your very feet.

Ahooga!
The Universe

Traction through Action

The key to charting a course, if you haven't noticed yet, lies in starting where you are, getting busy, and letting the course present itself, which will continue to become even clearer in the next two chapters.

Think of any good novel you've read or movie you've seen. A good storyteller can leave you dangling in suspense until the very end, until suddenly there's hope where there'd been none just moments before. From one moment to the next they can move you from hopelessness to clarity and then to celebration. In a way, although we can't quite fathom how we do it logistically with our brain, we're the amazing storytellers of our lives, and so long as we have a course to act on, the pages can turn and the story will present itself.

Like our spiritual selves, our energies and intentions are far wider reaching than we can comprehend, and even though we can't see around the bend in our lives any more than we can look ahead in a movie, for the efforts that we make today, options and possibilities are created for us tomorrow. And from the zenith of our hidden magnificence, that which we most want and love will be choreographed to present itself. All that's required is that you continue creating traction through action, day after day, starting from where you are—all of which becomes easiest when you understand your power and its source, while taking stock of your present situation, weighing your preferences, and physically moving.

Then the story never gets "stuck"; the pages keep turning, and your own inevitable celebration draws near until ultimately, the day dawns when you can look back on how the story unfolded, laughing to yourself, "Ohhhh! Of course! *Of course!* I needn't ever have worried!"

Summary Points

- You are here to be you, to let your desires take you wherever they may, to feel what has never been felt before.
- Change all your "What should I do?" questions to "What do I want to do?"
- If you already know what you want to do, go do it.
- If you don't know what you want to do but already have something to do, do that something even better.

* If you don't have anything to do and you don't know what you want to do, do anything and do it well.
* Where you are is never *who* you are.
* Give yourself a deadline to take steps on a new path; the sooner the better.

——————— Suggested Exercises ———————

Charting a Course

Where in your life are you now doing something because you felt you should do it, in spite of being drawn in other directions? Think about why you're doing what you do in:

* work or a career
* relationships
* home and family
* social life
* health and appearance

For the same areas above, consider charting a course in the days and months ahead that may allow you to change directions, beginning where you are, leaving behind the shoulds *and doing what you most want. What will you do? Where will you begin? When will you start?*

In the areas of your life where you'll continue doing much of what you now do, either temporarily or somewhat permanently, how can you begin to further master your tasks? How can you do them even better?

3

STEP THREE:

TAKE ACTION
AND DELEGATE

The third step involves taking action and delegating, differentiating between what you will do versus what you'll delegate to the Universe and life's magic. Here, we're going to be formulating a plan for creating the change you wish to experience. Business books talk about having a plan, as do most other how-to books, yet spiritual books often neglect this because, I presume, it seems too logical and practical. Yikes! Big mistake! I've met far too many newly "spiritually aware" people who could use a bit of old-school grounding!

Remember reading your first spiritual book? Perhaps it was *Illusions* or *Jonathan Livingston Seagull* by Richard Bach, or maybe it was *The Secret* by Rhonda Byrne. Do you remember that feeling you had, that euphoria and sense of liberation; the freedom and elation you felt when you *finally* grasped that you could indeed influence change in your life; that you were not alone; that there's a loving Universe conspiring on your behalf; that you've not been judged; that your future lies wide open and before you there are infinite possibilities for living life on your terms?

Too often people get such a "high" from reading these books and discovering the truth about what really makes the world go around that they think *their excitement alone* will change their lives.

It never does. This chapter is about *applying* these ancient truths to your everyday life and knowing what you can, should, and must delegate to the Universe and what you must do yourself—and why.

The Old-School versus New-School Approaches to Creating Life Changes

People of the old school were raised with the notion that to make a difference in the world, find their way, or achieve success, they had to do it alone and by the sweat of their brows. We can recognize old-school planners by the clichés that seem to roll off their tongues: "Opportunity only knocks once," "It's not what you know; it's who you know," "The early bird catches the worm," and so forth. People in this category are prone to messing with the *cursed hows* and are therefore carrying the weight of the world on their shoulders. Actually, this is what you and I were taught, being born into these less sophisticated times, and many of us were told, often explicitly, that struggle was the only path to achievement and success.

At the opposite end of the spectrum are the newly spiritual people who are waiting for the Universe to live their lives for them. They're so exhausted from carrying the world on their shoulders that once they hear the good news about the Universe and its magic, it's as if they pick up all their belongings, including the kitchen sink, run across the spectrum at full speed, and slam into the other wall, dropping everything with a big grin on their face, thinking *they don't have to do anything* in order to live the life of their dreams.

We may be spiritual beings having a human experience, but doesn't that make us both spiritual *and* human? Therefore, when it comes to deliberately creating change, we need to take both the spiritual and physical worlds into account. Or, if you prefer, this means we need to behave physically but with a spiritual awareness. We need to leverage the Universe and engage the magic with the fulcrum of our physical thoughts, words, and deeds. We want to find a happy medium between the old-school, take-action camp and the new school of "effortless manifesters." We need to be physical in order to be fully spiritual, and vice versa. When it comes to creating change, this means we must physically go out into the world in order to avail ourselves of life's spiritual principles, which are waiting to receive us for the thoughts we've begun thinking regarding the lives of our dreams.

> We may be spiritual beings having a human experience,
> but doesn't that make us both spiritual *and* human?
> Therefore, when it comes to deliberately creating
> change, we need to take both the spiritual and
> physical worlds into account.

Feeling Lucky?

Let's say, hypothetically, for illustrative purposes, that you believe in luck, and let's imagine for a moment that you believe you're about to enter the luckiest week of your entire life. You believe that this coming Monday, you'll be so lucky that it'll seem as if everything you touch turns to gold. And one more assumption for this lesson: let's also say that you fish for a living.

With the luckiest week of your life about to begin, when you go fishing Monday morning, would you go with one pole or many? You'd go with many, wouldn't you? And if you had a few days to prepare, you'd get a couple of boats for friends and family, and you'd clean out the sporting goods stores of all their fishing poles. You'd want to maximize your ability to take advantage of the luckiest week of your life, wouldn't you? You wouldn't walk out your front door Monday morning, look to the sky with arms in the air and shoulders hunched, and ask, "Where are the fish? Where are the fish? This is the luckiest week of my life!" No, it doesn't work that way with "luck," does it? In fact, even people naïve enough to believe in luck are wise enough to realize it'll do them no good if they don't *go out into the world to avail themselves of it!*

Now, there's no such thing as luck. But there's something better: It's this principle of *thoughts become things*. This principle can be counted on. It can be banked on. With this principle, anything can happen, *but* you have to fully understand its basic mechanics, which simply means, as with the fantasy of luck, it must be *physically engaged*. You must avail yourself of its magic. You must go out into the world so that your manifestations can reach you, so that the Universe can adjust your sails, and so that little serendipities, coincidences, and happy accidents can fall onto your path that wouldn't have otherwise if you had sat at home, waiting for a breakthrough.

A Plan of Action

Here's a little exercise for creating a plan of action that will leverage the Universe and engage the magic. It's such a simple plan (if "plan" is even the right word) that you can think of it and assemble your own version of it without even putting pen to paper, although I recommend writing it down your first time or two. Once you understand the exercise, you can do it when you're dozing off to sleep, walking the dog, or driving to work. This exercise gives you a tool for looking at your responsibilities versus those you *delegate to the Universe.*

The Triangle Exercise

In your mind's eye or with a piece of paper, imagine or draw a large triangle. This triangle will ultimately contain all the action steps necessary for a single dream of yours to come true, so it's important that the triangle is large enough for you to write many words and phrases inside of it.

Now imagine or draw a vertical line cutting the triangle in half from top to bottom. That means starting at the top of the triangle, where there's a point, and then imagining or drawing a straight line down to the center of the triangle's base. In the bottom left corner of the triangle, imagine or write your name, and in the bottom right corner of the triangle, imagine or write, "The Universe." (See the diagram on following page for guidance.)

You can create a triangle for any and all your dreams, such as for a new car, an improved relationship, a new career, direction, health, or anything you want. However, each dream will require its own triangle, so make sure you label each by writing your dream at the top of the triangle.

Your Side of the Triangle

On your side of the triangle, think of and/or write down *anything* and *everything* you can do to further your advancement toward the realization of your dream. Include all you can do physically, logically, and spiritually to achieve the goal at the top of the triangle.

I usually remind audiences that being logical and practical is highly overrated and that we need to begin using our intuition and instincts more, yet with our amazing brains and analytical

Mike Dooley

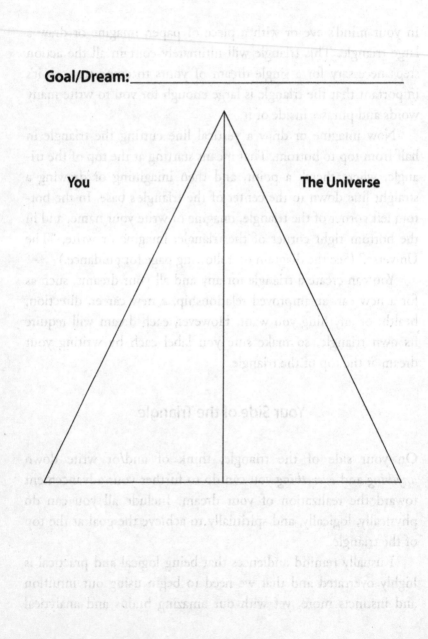

Goal/Dream: _____

You   The Universe

abilities, *sometimes* being logical and practical is being spiritual. Sometimes it allows you to stir up the magic.

For this exercise, what I mean by being logical and practical is this: on your side of the triangle, in addition to the other things you might consider, include some of the things that your peers would be doing to achieve the same goal, whether or not they know anything about the Universe and life's magic.

Another way to approach this logically goes back to what I said earlier: "If you don't know what it is you want to do, keep doing what you're doing, but do it better." If that applies to you, what were some of your answers in the last chapter's exercise that you could be doing even better? How could you be honing your skills and becoming a master of what's before you right now in your day-to-day life? These answers will make up the physical and logical part of our entries on your side, the left side of the triangle.

Here are some more ideas that may or may not apply to whatever it is you want, if you want to change or improve your career, work, or livelihood:

- If you're in sales, make more cold calls.
- Start or continue refining your education.
- Obtain licenses, certifications, websites, and/or business cards.
- Create a business plan.
- Actively seek or strategize to find new partners, investors, customers, and so on.
- Ask mentors for help.
- Read how-to books and success stories of those who have gone before you.
- Help others who want what you want (a great way to get a new perspective on your own situation).

For improving a relationship:

- Travel, cook, or learn to do something new together.
- Seek the advice of friends, family, or counselors to smooth out any issues.
- Try "date nights," or surprise your partner with new behavior.
- Revisit old places and activities that previously brought joy to the relationship.
- Talk to your partner more, in new ways—reaching out, compromising, or asking for help.
- Find others who are perhaps in a similar situation or form a support group.

For starting a new relationship:

- Be sure your friends are allies on your quest for love.
- Join dating services, online or otherwise.
- Get out more, especially to places where you could meet new people.
- Volunteer in your community, not only to help but to be available.
- Get a job (if not for the money, then to meet people).
- Choose a hobby and get involved with local groups who enjoy the same interests.

Spiritually speaking, no matter what you're after, here are some entries for your side of the triangle, *if* they appeal to you:

- Visualize every day (see tips on this in the next chapter).
- Join a spiritual community. Unity Churches and Centers for Spiritual Living Churches are in alignment with all I'm sharing about how to create change in your life.

- Read more books like this one, listen to audio programs, and attend seminars.
- Join meet-up and/or mastermind groups (or form your own).
- Begin or learn meditation, yoga, or other exercises that enhance peace of mind and physical well-being.
- Create a vision board and use other similar tools (again, see tips on this in the next chapter).

There's nothing new on these lists; what's new is what you'll bring to them—now that you understand how your baby steps will *enable* the Universe's giant steps on your behalf—because this can make all the difference.

The Universe's Side of the Triangle

On the other side of the triangle, think of the possible magic, miracles, serendipities, and happy accidents that you might experience, all of which would also help you advance toward the realization of your dream. This is where you're going to put in what the Universe can do for you. Some examples:

- Help you unexpectedly meet new people who can help you
- Give you a bright idea that will not only change your life but also the world
- Provide inspiration and motivation when you most need it
- Resolve inner conflicts
- Arrange circumstances to ease your journey
- Open your eyes to new possibilities
- Help you negotiate and transcend obstacles, tricky people, and other distractions that aren't serving you
- Hone your skills, improve talents, and instill confidence

- Accumulate physical resources and summon new opportunities
- Reveal your negative thinking and limiting beliefs
- And much more

Depending on what your dream is, add your own ideas to both sides of your triangle. See "My Side of the Triangle: Pitching to the Universe" and "The Universe's Side of the Triangle: The Home Runs" later in this chapter for more specific examples.

Doing All You Can, with What You've Got, from Where You Are

Once you've made your lists, take a look at both sides of the triangle and then realize that your doing *everything* on your side of the triangle would *never* be enough to make your dream come true without the Universe doing its part. Otherwise, you'd be flailing for the rest of your life. Similarly, if the Universe was ready to rock and roll on your behalf, able to do everything on its side of the triangle, yet you weren't doing your part, progress would be *impossible.* Here's the crux: *if* you don't do all you can, with what you have, from where you are (your side of the triangle), the Universe *cannot* do all it can for you. Again, yet rephrased, *if* you want the Universe to be able to do *all* it can, with all it has, from where it is, then you *must* do all you can, with what you have, from where you are.

> Here's the crux: *if* you don't do all you can,
> with what you have, from where you are,
> the Universe *cannot* do all it can for you.

We *do* have a choice as to just how much of the Universe we unleash, and it's based on the choice of how much action we take. The more we do, the more the Universe can do for us. Each of our baby steps increases exponentially the Universe's ability to reach us. This is not a call to work harder, longer, or more, more, more! It's a call to work smarter, be more aware, and better understand that physical steps in the direction of your dreams are necessary if you wish to see your *thoughts become things.*

The world we dream of living in literally morphs into place through subtle changes made possible when you're out and about, moving in the general direction of your dream. Not that you have to do *absolutely everything* possible to meet with stunning success; you don't. You probably only need to do very little! But since you don't know what that is, many baby steps are ideal, and by showing up often on many fronts, you'll likely choose the "right" ones sooner, thereby giving the Universe more "dots to connect" on your behalf.

By understanding that you're not alone, the pressure to craft your own breakthrough is lessened to the point that you can *finally* begin enjoying the journey, so much so that taking baby steps will be your new favorite thing to do and no longer a laborious task that only provides hit-or-miss successes.

A NOTE FROM THE UNIVERSE

Little tiny dreams require little tiny thoughts and little tiny steps.

Great big dreams require great big thoughts and little tiny steps.

Do I paint a clear picture?
The Universe

The Difference between the *Cursed Hows* and Taking Action

Whenever I begin talking about taking action in front of an audience, astute listeners begin questioning whether or not I'm contradicting my other message of "never messing with the *cursed hows*." And having gone over the simple triangle exercise we just went through with more than one hundred audiences in the past, I realize you, too, may be wondering: "Didn't you just have me create a list of *cursed hows*? Isn't my side of the triangle now filled with steps that will be limiting me and life's magic? Aren't I supposed to turn it *all* over to the Universe and just dwell upon the end result?" No—but these are excellent questions.

What differentiates a *how* from "doing all you can, with what you have, from where you are" is not *what you do* but *how you view what you're doing*.

If you're viewing the list on your side of the triangle as *how* you're going to make your big dream come true, they're *cursed hows*, and whether or not you realized this, you'd soon end up feeling like you're carrying the weight of the world on your shoulders as you move through the list. If, however, you view what you're doing as your way of inviting the Universe in on the action, then instead of seeing yourself as the one responsible for hitting the home run in your life, your action steps simply become pitches to the Universe, who can then hit the homer for you! This is exactly where you want to be. Don't let your action steps be seen as *how* you will hit the home run of your life; see them as pitches to a much wiser and far more powerful hitter: the Universe.

In this way, you're *not* messing with the *cursed hows*; instead, you're dancing life's dance, showing up, being reachable, and creating infinite possibilities for your dreams to come true. Plus, seen like this, if you throw a bad pitch every once in a while, no problem! Big deal! Who cares? Because you're going to continue pitching as you do all you can, with what you have, from where you are. This takes all the pressure off.

The More You Understand This, the More You'll Do

Keeping busy with lots of irons in the proverbial fire means you can stop sweating the details and detach from the outcome of any particular endeavor while *not* detaching from the overall grand design of your amazing new life. Now your salvation and future happiness do not have to be hinged, for example, to that book you wanted to write, that deal you wanted to close, or some other variety of *how* the big picture of your life *might* ultimately be assembled. If these things don't work out, again, no problem, big deal, who cares, because they were not necessarily how your dream was going to come true, anyway; they were simply pitches to the Universe. You don't know which pitch the Universe is going to smack out of the park, which is why you *continue* pitching. I see too many people who "throw one or two balls" and then sit on the sidelines saying, "How long is this going to take? What am I doing wrong? This isn't my dream job."

If you want to be a writer, it does no good to write one book and sit on the sidelines until the Universe makes it a bestseller. If you want to be a writer, by its very definition, you write. When you finish one project, you start another and you keep on writing, following your impulses, your instincts, your inner compass, so that you're always in a fluid state of motion—as any true writer would be. Then as you start soliciting and marketing your literary wares, the Universe can pick and choose from your entire portfolio, based upon the public's changing tastes, prevailing trends, and a host of other factors that all contribute to a bestseller.

Again, the distinction is in how you view what you do. The error I see in most people's thinking is that *because they believe in the magic*, they're out there trying to hit the home run. Well, do believe in the magic, but don't put all the pressure on every baby step you take! You *can't* know either where or when the Universe will enter your affairs—only that it will. So just pitch your pitches, take your baby steps, enjoy the journey, and prepare to be astounded.

You *can't* know either where or when the Universe will enter your affairs—only that it will. So just pitch your pitches, take your baby steps, enjoy the journey, and prepare to be astounded.

Once you've embraced this notion, anything and everything you do becomes much more relaxed. You can breathe easy. You don't have to freak out about being the early bird. You don't have to stress about who your connections are. You don't have to put yourself in the right place at the right time. The Universe will take care of all those things for you behind the scenes in the unseen, *as long as you are out there living your life*—even when those first baby steps seem like they're a million miles from the life of your dreams. They certainly were in my experience eleven years ago.

How It Worked for Me

My own leveraging the Universe and engaging the magic story centers around the creation of *Infinite Possibilities*, the original audio program that culminated in the *New York Times* bestselling book of the same name, before diverging into many more exciting tangents. As you now know, eleven years ago, Mom, Andy, and I had just wrapped up our ten-year adventure in the T-shirt and gift business. During our last three years together, all our financial trends were in a steep decline. After having tried virtually everything to reverse this slide to no avail, with our three stores and warehouse leases all fortuitously coming to a near simultaneous end, Andy, Mom, and I decided to liquidate the remaining inventory, split the remaining cash, and let the adventure go. Doing so would enable us each to have enough money to coast for a few years while we figured out our own lives and, not so coincidentally, avoid going down with our "sinking ship."

The "Train Wreck"

And so began the most difficult and humbling and scariest time of my life. I was faced with starting over—yet I didn't even know what or where to start. I had zero career momentum, and though I had money, I also had a mortgage many times greater! That year, I'd fall asleep at night and wake up covered in sweat for two reasons: First, I'd wonder, "What did I do that I shouldn't have done? What *didn't* I do that I *should've* done? How did this happen to me *of all people*?!" Second, I'd become such a frightened miser that I wouldn't allow myself to run my home's air-conditioning below 82 degrees—in Florida!

I remember vividly the typical tropical thunderstorms brewing that summer, with their billowing white cumulonimbus clouds towering seven miles high and undersides as dark as night. The winds would pick up in great sudden gusts. The lightning would crackle and flash, and thunder would explode overhead and roll off into the distance. For the first time in my life, just the sight of these storms approaching physically scared me. It was as if they were reminding me of how precarious my life seemed at the time, and I was afraid that at any moment I might be helplessly blown into oblivion.

During my darkest moments I'd sometimes wonder to myself, "Gosh, with the great run I had at Price Waterhouse, and with all the fun Andy, Mom, and I had traveling around the world selling T-shirts, maybe this is the way my life was 'supposed' to go. Maybe now I need to see how everyone else lives. Maybe the best of my life is behind me and forever more I'll be telling stories about Hong Kong, Price Waterhouse, and selling T-shirts from Tokyo to Helsinki."

Yet from this "train wreck" my phoenix rose, as it *always* does when we choose to press on. Ironically, within just a few years of the "calamity," and to this day, I'm *still* asking the question I used to ask on those sweaty Florida nights: *"How did this happen to me?"* Yet now when I ask, it's for an entirely different reason than before. And now I know the answer: *I leveraged the Universe and engaged life's magic.*

**Yet from this "train wreck" my phoenix rose,
as it *always* does when we choose to press on.**

In spite of my fears, the worrying morning, noon, and night, and my negative behavior—not running my air conditioner, discontinuing my cable television service, and living with poverty consciousness—thinking what I knew to think, saying what I knew to say, and doing what I knew to do was enough to tap into my own natural inclination to succeed, prosper, and, indeed, thrive.

And the "train wreck"? There wasn't one! I'll explain that in chapter 5, "Align Your Beliefs."

My Side of the Triangle: Pitching to the Universe

While at the time I couldn't explain how I had created the seeming mess I was in, as I spelled out earlier, you don't have to know how you got where you are in order to move forward. *Thoughts become things.* Know where you want to go (at least generally)—and start going. If you don't know where you want to go, start going somewhere—anywhere!

What follows is a lengthy review of all I did: what seemingly failed and what engaged life's magic. I share this in such detail so that you can fully understand the nitty-gritty nuances, fear, and setbacks I encountered and so that you can perhaps see how "real" my struggle was, find parallels in your own journey, and be reminded that sometimes taking one or two steps back is exactly the formula for the type of success you're after.

What I Wouldn't Do

While I didn't know where I wanted to go specifically, other than in the direction of reinventing myself, I was willing to do *almost* anything to get there, wherever "there" was. What I *wasn't* willing to do anymore, however, was sell products, even though I knew that by setting some conditions like that, I'd be placing limits on life's magic. Still, we *are* entitled to draw some lines. It is, after all, our life.

I made another vow: I would not write a book. The reason: during the T-shirt/gift days, for a couple of summers, I spent virtually every single weekend sequestered in my home, writing a book—for all the wrong reasons. It was a *cursed how*: trying to write a book that would set me free in life and surround me in wealth and abundance. The book was to be titled *The Time-Space Continuum*. It was very objective and dry, about understanding

Mike Dooley

our beliefs, imaginations, the actions we take, and the realities we live in. There wasn't a single story or an analogy in it. Yet it wasn't until the end of that process, two years later, that I realized the book I had written wasn't sellable; in fact, it was hardly readable, and I felt like I had thrown away a chunk of my life by insisting, "I can do this."

In hindsight, of course, it was a valuable lesson. I was doing something for the wrong reasons, and the results it produced were not pleasing, nor did they enable me to achieve the objective I had set out to achieve. With the "must do" mind-set, and my attachment to this lone endeavor being my only salvation, I was not able to master what was before me. The pressure was far too great, and the weight of the world made for really terrible penmanship.

What I Would Do

Other than these simple prohibitions, I was ready to roll up my sleeves and literally do whatever it took. Here's a list of what transpired in the following year, told from the point of view of how I leveraged the Universe and engaged life's magic. I'd also like to point out that most of the following things I did were done simultaneously, meaning I did not "knock on one door to see if anyone was home" before proceeding to the next door:

Polished off my accountant's résumé. Well, we all know how that went, as described in the last chapter! No job prospects meant win-win for me and the world, as in, "think again."

I continued my creative writing. I also shared this story earlier, and what began as a weekly "Monday Morning

Motivator" soon turned into a daily email called "Silver Bullets." After *nine months* of "Silver Bullets," wanting to change the name (for rather obvious reasons) but not knowing to what, I was also haunted by a sense that I could say more, and perhaps with added creditability, if I wrote from the perspective of "the Universe."

I created a website. I transformed the old T-shirt and gift company's site into TUT's Adventurers Club, which would serve as a resource for "life adventurers."

I sold "Survival Kits." In spite of swearing off products, neither the website nor the emailings were bringing in a dime. Plus, I still had some inventory left over from the T-shirt days that I could combine into a little gift package, which I dubbed "Survival Kits" for the adventure of life! What a fun idea, huh? I sold about thirty the first week and then about three in the following month. Not quite a living.

I hosted my own eCards. By exploring the internet and studying the meager statistics for my humble website, I realized that a particular website was sending a lot of traffic my way. I approached the owners in gratitude and with questions, and my whole world changed—though not in the way I'd thought it would and not nearly as fast.

On the surface, their site was simply one that hosted a collection of free, inspirational eCards that were a combination of their art and other people's sayings, poems, and quotes—from the living (like me!) and the dead (like Abraham Lincoln). On the two or three eCards that used my quotes (poems from our T-shirt days), they gave credit to tut.com (hence the traffic they were sending my way). Beneath the surface, they were a money-making machine, earning upwards of $15,000 per month! (They did point out, however, that with the recent advent of the dot-com bubble burst, their earnings were on the decline. Hey, I could handle almost any kind of decline from $15,000 per month, I thought!)

They were online pioneers in viral marketing—which sounds rather distasteful, but it's simply a form of word-of-mouth advertising that promotes an idea or, in this case, a website or eCard. For instance, if someone enjoyed an eCard, that person might send it to ten friends, and each friend might tell ten more friends. That's viral marketing.

On every confirmation page that followed the sending of an eCard, there would be an advertising banner from a big company like Exxon Mobil, Delta Air Lines, or a credit card company. Some of these advertisers were paying upwards of a dollar *per click* to their hosts for the traffic, though most paid from 5 to 25 cents and others, like the credit card companies, were paying up to $25 per conversion if someone clicked the banner you were hosting and subsequently applied for a credit card!

I asked for help! When you're doing all you can, with what you have, from where you are, with regard to your side of the triangle, *always* include asking questions, asking for help, and approaching people who are doing what you might want to be doing and have already blazed a trail. Time and again, in all my life's pursuits, whether as an accountant, retailer, or budding speaker, I've not only asked for help but have been repeatedly astounded at how willing and helpful others have been in rendering assistance to a complete stranger. In this case, my new viral marketing friends graciously explained *everything* they and many others at the time were doing, and encouraged me to do the same. They shared their entire business model with me, including where to go for banners, which essentially taught me affiliate marketing, the other name for what they were doing (they were "affiliates" of the companies whose banners they hosted).

WOW! I was on fire with excitement! I had ten years' worth of poems from our T-shirt days, most of which were perfect for eCards! I spent three months in a delirious work frenzy, and I was singing every day! It seemed to me that the Universe had conspired, and this boondoggle I was about to embark on was "meant to be." By the end of the three months, however, sad to say, the internet bubble had *completely* burst, and I never made more than $100 in a month on my eCards. The only silver lining to the story, at that point, was that my eCards did indeed become very popular. It's just that they truly were free, even beneath the surface.

❊ TIME OUT ❊

Two little side notes before I resume the story: First, *nothing* is meant to be! We are creators, and we create with our focus. There are no preconditions, no destinies, no caveats. If something—anything—were meant to be, it would rob us of our freedom, power, and responsibilities to discover this truth. Sure, some things feel good, and our hunches and instincts tell us to pounce, in which case, pounce! But don't drop everything in their pursuit, unless that, too, feels good (and works with your overall approach and sense of responsibilities), but don't hinge your happiness on their outcome.

Second, just because something doesn't work out the way you'd thought it would doesn't mean it didn't work out in other ways. It may have worked out in even better ways that you've yet to realize.

❋ ❋ ❋

Continuing my story:

I joined Toastmasters. In order to create yet another avenue for possible success, and for the joy I've always felt when speaking (*strictly* to family and friends!) about the nature of reality, I considered making myself available to the world as a professional speaker. Yet speaking before an audience terrified me. Many years earlier, in the embarrassment of a lifetime, I drew a total blank midsentence in front of three dozen PW clients, partners, and peers. So to test the waters this time I joined Toastmasters, a self-improvement organization that helps new speakers get a handle on their fear of public speaking. There I discovered that no matter how terrified I was (and I was a mess), I could still get my point across—something I didn't know until joining. S-l-o-w-l-y, I improved one speech after another on the topics of life, dreams, and happiness. I didn't just talk about my dogs and planting trees (well, only a few times); I joined Toastmasters to do the best I could with what I had, given my dream of a career resurrection, and that naturally meant speaking about the kinds of things that I might be called upon to one day speak about.

One year into my membership, I branched out, speaking at middle schools, Unity Churches, and Rotary Clubs—all for free (though the entire ordeal still terrified me)—and I remained a member of Toastmasters for seven years.

I asked for more help! I also started attending National Speakers Association (NSA) meetings in Lakeland, Florida. The NSA is the professional body for speakers in the United States. I wasn't allowed to join, since I wasn't a professional speaker, but I was allowed to attend the meetings as a paying guest, and because the meetings were like workshops for speakers, I learned tons and met some great people. One of them was the chapter president, who, it turned out, also lived in Orlando. Following my own earlier advice (to find people who are doing what you want to be doing), I decided to give him a call one day and *ask for help*. "Absolutely!" was his reply.

We spent three hours together one night over a couple of beers, during which we talked about *nothing* but how *he* could put eCards on his website so that he could have the kind of banner revenue that I was hoping for.

I drove home that evening thinking, "You know, maybe speaking isn't for me." But a few days later he called me. "Mike, you've got a database of a few thousand people that you send your emails to, and I've got a database of a few thousand people that I send mine to. And I have a friend who knows everything about internet marketing who's suggested to me that I create an audio program to be sold as a subscription, with one recording to be released each month in the coming year, and I'd love to have you as my partner. We could offer the program to our subscribers before we even create it, and the whole thing can be recorded onto a little Sony MiniDisc Walkman for future editing and replication!" I couldn't believe it. I was floored that the president of the local NSA chapter would call and ask *me* to partner with him!

Then came *Infinite Possibilities.* I promptly abandoned the two vows I had made about no products and no books because his offer was an entirely unforeseeable set of circumstances. Besides, it wouldn't really be a book, and I'd have a partner. I came up with the title, *Infinite Possibilities: The Art of Living Your Dreams* ("Dang, I need to listen to that program," I secretly thought to myself), and my partner loved it too.

A few weeks later, by the end of the day that we announced it to our two respective email lists, I had earned $5,000 in subscriptions, but my partner had no sales. Comparing notes afterwards, he said, "Since you've done so well, I don't feel right about splitting the proceeds. Why don't you go ahead and do your version of *Infinite Possibilities* and I'll do mine?"

Shock quickly turned to elation! It became the happiest moment of a very happy day for two reasons: First, by that time, I just *knew* I could pull this project off alone, and second, I was *one full year* into my involuntary "nonprofit" venture, each month of which had peeled away very slowly while my resources dwindled. My bank statement every month had shown lots of debits and no credits! I couldn't have asked for anything better at that point.

Then my elation turned to panic! January 1, the promised mailing date for the first installment of *Infinite Possibilities*, was just a few weeks away, and I had nothing to mail! In my scramble, can you guess where I decided the first hour of *Infinite Possibilities* would come from? I ended up cutting, splicing, and merging my first year's worth of Toastmasters speeches.

Within three days, I had the first seventy minutes recorded. And for February's recording, I ended up using "Beliefs," chapter 2 of my long-ago filed away and almost forgotten *The Time-Space Continuum*, spiced up with some stories and analogies, of course. And virtually every month after that, I was able to draw from my old book to beef up the content, while adding extra bits to make it more interesting. It was amazing.

The Universe's Side of the Triangle: The Home Runs

This entire twelve-month journey that culminated in creating and selling *Infinite Possibilities* illustrates what I'm talking about when I say do all you can, with what you have, from where you are, even if it doesn't make perfect sense. Little I did made sense on its own, yet it all ultimately coalesced into something that exceeded my every expectation.

Do all you can, with what you have, from where you are, even if it doesn't make perfect sense.

My friends likely thought I was nuts, working on one little project after another, some with no revenue-stream potential, when I *should* have been out pounding the pavement, getting a "real job." I was writing for free, building a website for free, and speaking for free. My eCards and "Survival Kits" bombed. Then suddenly—an overnight success? Hardly!

Yet it was as if every little thing I did that year was a failure. Every door I knocked on, every stone I turned over—all of it made possible my being touched by life's magic. Here's what the Universe did for me, made possible by my "pitches."

What the Universe Did for Me

* I achieved clarity with regard to returning to the corporate world.
* I *discovered* creative writing, teaching, and public speaking.
* My old manuscript, *The Time-Space Continuum*, and all the time invested in the book those two summers were salvaged.
* My Toastmasters experience provided the program's content and eventually led to speaking professionally, albeit another *year* later.
* My self-imposed parameters of no products and no books were shattered! Attending the NSA meetings and asking for help as a speaker made it possible for the Universe to seemingly jump into some guy's body (a complete stranger to me) and possess him with the mission "to get Mike Dooley past his self-imposed limits of 'no book and no product,' and while you're at it, boost his self-confidence! Once achieved, get the heck out of Dodge!" And that's exactly what happened.
* My "Survival Kits," while never a success, had at least gotten me credit-card enabled and proficient with internet retailing.
* The eCards and viral/affiliate marketing I had learned became invaluable very quickly. During the first year of sales, beyond selling to my own list, they were almost exclusively

how I sold *Infinite Possibilities* to the public at large. First, I changed out the banners from Delta Air Lines and other companies with ones for *Infinite Possibilities*, and then I aggressively pursued new affiliates.

Where Exactly Was the Universe?

Does all this sound like the simple and inevitable payoff for hard work? Are you kidding? We live in a *dream* world! Chance, coincidence, and luck are old-school concepts for the naïve or foolish. Here our *thoughts become things*! See "The Home Runs" section that follows for the measured "payoff" of the Universe catching up with my efforts, and then consider how many hopeful writers and speakers there are in the United States, or even the world, who dream of creating bestselling books, traveling globally, and speaking to thousands. Haven't a good many of them worked *at least* as hard as I did, if not much harder, yet without the same payoffs I found? *Why should I have succeeded?*

I succeeded, and so will you, because we:

1. Possess a solid understanding of our power (whether you ascribe it to God or yourself is unimportant), without diluting it or blocking it with uncertainties and doubt.

2. Consistently dream of getting "more" from life, without contradicting ourselves (see chapter 5, "Align Your Beliefs," for help with this).

3. Take consistent action in the direction of our dreams, doing something daily—anything—to make us available to life's magic.

With this modicum of input for direction, the entire Universe and all its magic are leveraged and engaged. It knows how to make your dreams come true. It's just that until now, you thought it was all your responsibility. Again, our inclination is to thrive (the rationale for which is explained at length in *Infinite Possibilities*). In this world, it's as if we summon legions in the unseen to do our bidding and conspire on our behalf—*if we understand, hold on to the dream, and stay the course.*

In my story, it was as if *everything* I had done—all those seemingly feeble baby steps—lent themselves, in some way, to bringing the Universe and life's magic to bear, making possible the creation and selling of *Infinite Possibilities* and much more. Those little steps *made possible* far more than I could have even imagined at that time eleven years ago, when I was frightened of thunderstorms! Truly, the year leading up to the release of *Infinite Possibilities* as an audio program was a year jam-packed with hidden miracles. And they haven't stopped since.

The Home Runs

* Making and selling *Infinite Possibilities* was not only fun and fulfilling (though loaded with challenges), but it also made more than enough money to fund everything else I was to do for the following seven years.
* *Infinite Possibilities* gave me creditability as a budding speaker in the years that followed its release. It ultimately comprised twelve hours of the best I had to offer.
* I began to publicize my little Unity Church speeches in advance, just to my subscribers, which, unbeknownst to me, *got the attention of people in need of speakers!* I was invited to speak in Holland and then in London, launching my first

world tour, which gave me the confidence and ability to reach out to other cities, from Australia to Switzerland, to host my own events in the next year.

* My first world tour led to my second world tour, which led to another, and has offered me opportunities to speak in Auckland, Moscow, Johannesburg, and Istanbul, just to name a few places.

* My daily *Notes from the Universe* continues to this day, with more than two thousand written. These mailings are how Rhonda Byrne found me, and they impressed her enough for her to purchase *Infinite Possibilities* for her iPod long before inviting me to be in *The Secret.*

* Being in *The Secret* brought my work to the attention of publishers (they're sometimes slow to pick up on trends!), this book being the ninth released in the last four years.

* When *Infinite Possibilities* was later published as a book, it debuted on the *New York Times* bestsellers list.

* Having a *New York Times* bestseller got the attention of foreign publishers, who have now published a wide selection of my books in twenty-five languages, and counting.

* I now own a gorgeous office space in Orlando (in a building called "Heaven," quite appropriately), home to TUT World Headquarters, with a full-time staff of five amazing people. Together, we administer the daily emailings to a growing community of four hundred thousand people, operate a website that contains thousands of web pages, run a retail business with loads of inspirational products, from jewelry to DVDs, orchestrate my world tours, and run our nonprofit "Gifts from the Universe" project, which has raised more than $300,000 for various charities and for which I speak to inmates several times a month at

the Orange County (Florida) jail, informing them of life's magic and their powers.

Better still, there's all that's presently happening in the *unseen*! No, I haven't a clue as to what, but I know it's happening! Just because we can't yet see something happening, as my tale hopefully evidenced, doesn't mean it's not happening—both for me *and you*—so long as we keep dreaming and taking baby steps, in spite of not knowing where they may land or how they may be used later.

Finally, in case there's any doubt, and as I said earlier, *I love my life*—socially, romantically, and playfully—every bit as much as professionally.

Let the Universe Connect the Dots

Another analogy I like to share for what happens in all our lives when we move toward a dream with lots of action can be summed up in this *Note*:

A NOTE FROM THE UNIVERSE

Hold it! Stop! No! No! No!

Thinking about "how," weren't you? "How are you going to get from here to there?" kind of thoughts—the cursed hows. Bummer, huh?

There's nothing quite as demoralizing in the human experience as trying to use your brain to map the unseen, because immediately you sense it's hopeless—and you're right!

You can't map the unseen!

But I can.

You just need to define "there" and get busy doing what you can in every direction that feels right, though insisting upon none. Do the logical things (like knocking on doors and turning over stones). Do the spiritual things (like visualizing and taking catnaps). And leave the accidents, coincidences, and spontaneous illumination to me.

In a way, it's almost like throwing paint on the wall and then trusting me to connect the dots. Because I will, and the resulting masterpiece will blow you away. I promise.

After all, who do you think gave the Mona Lisa her smile?

Cheese,
The Universe

P.S. Hey, cool about the catnaps, huh? Made me think of you.

And literally, after dipping your hands in paint buckets and flinging paint all over the walls—a metaphor for taking action, even when it doesn't make physical sense—you'll become so engrossed with what you're doing, you won't even notice what's being created in front of you, until one day, when you stop to catch your breath and glance at your creation, you'll find the most stunning masterpiece you've ever witnessed. It'll be as if the Universe snuck onto the scene when you were busy doing all you could with what you had and connected the dots for you—as if, to your utter amazement, *every single dot*, no matter how stray, was critically important to the whole, each one, no matter how errant, carefully used by Divine Intelligence.

Similarly, you'll wake up one morning, look around, and wonder what role you played—shrouded in doubt and apprehension and taking puny little baby steps—to bring about the amazing life you'll then be living.

Just Like Sailing

Imagine that you own a magnificent yacht and that you're about to go on a wonderful sailing voyage. You can bring as many friends as you want and all your favorite DVDs, CDs, food, and drinks. Let's say it's docked in San Diego, and you've decided to go to Tahiti—and maybe beyond. How far would you and your friends get if all you did once you got on board was go down in the berth and get really excited about the trip? Nowhere. Watching *The Secret* together a thousand times wouldn't budge that boat.

The only way you would ever get to Tahiti is if you first took the simplest, most basic steps. You *must* untie the boat from the dock. You *must* use the little putt-putt engine to get out of the harbor. And then, "woe is me," you *must* hoist that big five-hundred-pound sail with the help of machinery and friends so that then, *and only then*, the magical winds of the Universe can fill your sails and take you to any port of call on this crystal blue gem we live upon. The hard part is done for us *if, and only if,* we do the little stuff, putting us within reach of life's magic. Our job is *simple*!

But if we overanalyze it, we may psyche ourselves out. After all, hoisting the sails won't land you in Tahiti. "Hey, my instructor said we could go anywhere, but it's not working for me. I must have invisible limiting beliefs. Maybe I don't think I'm worthy enough. Maybe it's not in my best interests. Maybe I was bad in a past life." Nonsense! It *does* work for you! You *are* worthy enough! But you must *continue* to do your part, consistently, daily, no matter how things appear. And then—maybe not overnight, maybe it'll take a few years—*you'll* be the one teaching others how all this stuff works.

The Real Reason the Early Bird Catches the Worm

It's easy to see the Universe and its magic in the lives of people who are very successful. I see this in successful entrepreneurs I know. They might not know a lick about the Universe and life's magic, yet somehow they know to do the most basic, fundamental things that will predispose them to miraculous circumstances. The reason, however, that they're so successful, apart from having a goal and a vision, is because they have this glint in their eye that says they are committed to doing whatever it takes. They're automatically doing everything they can, with what they have, from where they are, and they're not too proud to humble themselves with menial work, particularly in the beginning of their journey.

When I graduated from high school and went to college with the rest of my peers, I had one boyhood friend who stayed back and went into the restaurant business, bussing tables. Every spring break and holiday when I'd go home to visit, he and I would get together and trade stories. It was actually a bit uncomfortable for both of us. He felt left behind, as the rest of his friends were off on college adventures, poised to "conquer the world."

One day, on a vacation from school, my other friends and I were hanging out with him and discovered that he had left the restaurant business. He had gotten into sales, selling ladders. "Nice going! Congratulations! The sky is the limit!" we chimed, trying to be positive about his new direction in life—a ladder salesman. After receiving the warm wishes, he stopped us. He wanted to show us his sales pitch. Humoring him, we agreed.

Talk about enthused! Talk about mastering what's before you! When his ten-minute demonstration was done, not only did we all *seriously* want to buy one of his ladders, but we also all wanted to join him in business! So did everyone he pitched these ladders to. He was "tearing things up" at fire stations and school boards across the entire state of Florida! By the time of my next visit home, he had become the *number one* ladder salesman in the United States. This friend later went on to scaffolding (a natural extension—pardon the pun)! He began supplying high-rise contractors in Florida's booming office construction bonanza! The last I heard, many years later, in addition to his ladder and scaffolding business, he had gotten back into the restaurant business, this time as a proprietor, and his plans were to start franchising. His success has been unending, far exceeding what many of us "more fortunate" college grads have yet to find, and if I had to say what made him so successful, it was his willingness to do all he could, with what he had, from where he was.

The real reason the early bird catches the worm is not because they're early but because they're there; *they showed up*, and the Universe provided. As I implied at the outset of this chapter, the simple action plan you must create and follow after having a dream entails little more than being physically available. It means you must humbly get out into the world, *go*, show up, *without worrying about or insisting upon the hows*, delegating them to life's magic.

A NOTE FROM THE UNIVERSE

It's true; the early bird gets the worm.

So does the late bird and the bird in between.
Because by design, there are always more than enough worms.

In fact, the only bird that doesn't get a worm
is the bird that doesn't go out to get one.

Oh, to be alive!
The Universe

"Read My Lips"

To ensure that nothing was misunderstood here, and so that I don't ever read somewhere on the internet that "Mike Dooley promotes following your heart and just trusting the Universe," let me clearly share that this is *not* what I just promoted. More than anything else, this chapter has been about taking action—and to that end, knowing what to be concerned with versus what to delegate to life's magic, being willing to physically do *anything and everything* possible to see your dream come true, which includes mixing in some logic as you do all you can, with what you have, from where you are, using your heart and your brain to physically put yourself on a path that will, to the best of your knowledge and abilities at the time, in all regards (including financially), help you meet your responsibilities and achieve your dreams.

With all the doors I knocked upon, I was painfully aware that I was running out of money, so I wasn't going to knock on a door that had no possibility of generating cash. In a sense, you might say that I was working within my belief system without really naming those beliefs. I wasn't insisting that water come from stone. *Because I was in a position to coast*, I was willing to go down these tried-and-true business paths of speaking, writing, and all the others, albeit in some unconventional ways and without money for a stretch. Had I been in a different position and had I been desperate for cash or had bills come due that I couldn't pay, I can assure you that I would have taken a job at the local pizzeria if necessary, or would have started preparing tax returns for H&R Block—viewing such concessions as steps that would have enabled me to simultaneously follow my heart, as I would have then been able to afford doing my "nonprofit" work, though perhaps scaled back a bit.

And the reason for all the emphasis on action is because taking it, coupled with understanding your reality and having at least general wishes and intents, is exactly how to leverage the Universe and engage life's magic.

--------- **Summary Points** ---------

* Being excited about life's magic is never enough to change your life; you must put yourself within its reach by taking action.
* Find a happy medium between the old-school "take-action" camp and the new-school "effortless-manifesters" camp.
* You need to physically engage the world in order to be fully spiritual, and vice versa.
* The only way to *fully* engage the Universe is to fully engage yourself by doing all you can, with what you have, from where you are.
* Sometimes getting logical is the most spiritual thing you can do.
* The reason for taking action is to get the Universe in on the game.

The Triangle Exercise

Create your own triangle exercises for your biggest dreams in the key areas of your life in which you'd like to create change. Follow the format of the diagram discussed earlier in this chapter on page 52.

4

STEP FOUR:

LEVERAGE
THE UNIVERSE

What you think, say, and do are your fulcrums for life's magic: the pivot points upon which the Universe and life's magic are leveraged. They're what enable you to do the least to get the most, as your every thought, word, and deed is amplified in the unseen to such a degree that they physically return as future manifestations. In fact, if you think about it, you'll quickly realize that in life you have *nothing* but your thoughts, words, and deeds as your only points of contact with the Universe. Of course, our feelings, intentions, and desires are mighty factors as well, but they are all revealed by (or can be installed by) using our thoughts, words, and deeds. And so it becomes evident that to really get a leg up on creating change, these points must be used as wisely and vigilantly as possible.

To spark real change in our lives, we want to be defensively aware of old habits and mannerisms so that we're not unwittingly entertaining thoughts, words, and deeds that don't serve us, while at the same time going on the offensive to think, say, and do things that are specifically designed to give us the most "bang for our buck." In this step, I'm going to talk about working with thoughts, words, and deeds in both lights: defensively and offensively.

A Note from the Universe

A little-known secret concerning life in the jungles of time and space is that however far you reach, you will go further. However great your dreams, they will be grander. And however much you love, you will be loved much more.

We call it the Law of Increasing Returns.

Love you much more,
The Universe

Working with Your Thoughts

Every time-space manifestation starts in thought, and every thought starts with your choice to think it, sometimes more consciously than others, yet we are unquestionably their source. And as we come to learn of their phenomenal power, so, too, do we come to learn of our enormous responsibility—a responsibility that is not nearly as daunting as it first seems, given our natural-born optimism and our inclination to succeed, yet a responsibility nonetheless.

Being on the Defense

First, let's talk about thoughts from a defensive perspective. There's a book title I once saw: *You Can't Afford the Luxury of a Negative Thought*, and on the plane of manifestation where we live, this title pretty much sums things up! As I've explained in the book edition of *Infinite Possibilities*, it's as if our positive thoughts are ten thousand times more powerful than our negative thoughts.

Still, a negative thought, like all our thoughts, literally goes out into the unseen, rearranging the players and circumstances of our lives as they strive to become the things and events of the future. Obviously it doesn't serve us to think negatively, bemoan the past, or comfort ourselves by wallowing in sad memories.

Being defensive with your thoughts is pretty easy, and it comes automatically with simply being aware, perhaps finally, of the true power of our thoughts, and that they do, in fact, eventually become the things and events of your life. It's somewhat like having antivirus software on your computer. You can forget that it's there for weeks, months, or years until the day you've got a virus. Suddenly, your antivirus software interrupts whatever you're doing and tells you that your system has been infected. Being defensive with your thoughts is similar in that you don't have to write to-do notes every morning, reminding yourself to monitor the thoughts you're choosing! *Just being aware* of this principle and its almighty effect in your life and realizing that dwelling on unpleasant things merely perpetuates their existence in your life is generally enough to tip you off, and it'll help you consciously catch yourself when your thinking takes a dive. If you do start feeling sorry for yourself, from this day forward, do your best to stop and replace those thoughts with something that will serve you and your progress toward your dreams.

I'm *not* saying that whenever you have a negative or fearful thought that you should pretend it doesn't exist. On the contrary, hold that negative, limiting, fearful thought up to the light of truth. If you're worried about money and your ability to bring more of it into your life in the future, hold that thought up to the truth that you are an unlimited being of light for whom all things are possible, while taking into consideration all else I've shared with you. Remind yourself that this world is a world of illusions—

illusions that you can change. And remember that what one person has done, whether it's making a comeback or scaling the tallest heights, all are able to do.

Holding your thoughts up to the light of truth will often be enough to dispel them, from which point you can replace them with other thoughts that serve you. This is relatively easy, and with a little bit of persistence, you'll find you get better and better at it.

Runaway Trains of Negative Thinking

On the occasions fear or worry overcome you, relax! I used to panic whenever negativity coursed through my mind, thinking I was doomed because of this principle of *thoughts become things*, but I discovered something long ago when I thought I was being fired at PW: while there are indeed times in all our lives when we simply *cannot* stop our runaway trains of fear or negativity, at all times we are free and able to simultaneously start a new train running.

Let the negativity train run, and run, and run, while doing your best not to encourage it, but at least once a day, sit down and think some happy and inspiring thoughts. Visualize those thoughts too, if that suits you. (I'll talk about how in just a moment.) Now, if your crisis-inspired negativity has been like mine, even during these sacred sessions of happy thinking, *you will still worry about your current "crisis"*! That's OK. Stick with the program. Do your best, however difficult it may seem, to sit still for five minutes or so and imagine positive outcomes to whatever the crisis may be, *or go beyond the crisis* and imagine calm seas and gentle breezes with a smile on your face. To this day, this little drill has seen me through every crisis-inspired, negative-thinking runaway train that has ever commandeered my mind.

How does this work? Again, due to our inclination to thrive, our very reason for being in time and space, it's *as if* our positive thoughts are *at least* ten thousand times more powerful than our negative thoughts. Plus, in addition to your new five minutes of "a new train running," you will surely be doing all else you can in word and deed, thereby bringing the entire Universe to bear—*and your combined efforts will always be enough to turn the tide.*

Going on the Offense

Going on the offense with your thoughts is also easy. In one word: visualize. There is little else you can do with such minimal effort in such a short span of time that will do so much to spark great changes in your life. If you've read any of my other work, it may seem that I'm repeating myself to bring up visualizing again, yet it's just too great a tool to ever omit for new readers, and for the rest of us, it's too easy to take for granted the massive changes visualizing can spark.

Creative Visualization

In *Manifesting Change* I shared my six guidelines for Creative Visualization. The next few pages offer a summary, with fewer explanations and rationale. These guidelines are ones I follow as closely as possible when I visualize, usually Monday through Friday, before heading to the office in the morning (I take the weekends off!). These are not rules, just suggestions. Perhaps you can mix in your own preferences and considerations once you get the hang of it.

Visualization Guidelines

1. *Visualize once a day.* No more is needed. Plus, you don't want to end up dwelling in some future fantasy world while missing out on your already amazing life.

2. *Visualize no longer than five to ten minutes at a time.* Again, no more is needed; I usually set a timer for four minutes. Plus, if you do it longer, you run the risk of daydreaming and drawing the false conclusion that you aren't capable of visualizing.

3. *Imagine every conceivable detail.* Sights, sounds, colors, textures, aromas—make these scenes in your mind's eye as real and vivid as possible. If you can't form images when you visualize, skip to the next guideline.

4. *Feel the emotion.* Emotion is the turbocharger of *thoughts becoming things.* If you want fast change in your life, feel the joy when you visualize! If you can't form images when you visualize, feeling joy is your ticket. Skip straight to this most important detail of all. Emotional joy is what we're all really after anyway, so why not cut to the chase when you visualize?

5. *Put yourself in the picture.* Let it be you and your life that you're imagining, not glossy pictures with other people in them. To help with this, touch your surroundings in your imagination, hear the music, and see the expressions of happy faces reacting to you and your presence.

6. *Dwell from the end result—or beyond.* In other words, when visualizing, never, ever think about the *cursed hows.*

Create a scene or a feeling that implies you have *already* arrived at the place of your dreams.

How to Focus When Wanting More Than One Thing

One question that I hear from a lot of people is, "If I'm only supposed to visualize once a day for five or ten minutes, yet I want to effect change in every area of my life, how do I squeeze it all in?" There's no single answer, and again, there are no *rules* to visualizing, but here are a couple of approaches that might help when you're overwhelmed by the multitude of changes you want to manifest.

Happiness

The first approach, and perhaps most effective, is again to focus on joy. Imagine yourself feeling really good. It doesn't matter *what* you're thinking about—just be happy because, as I said in the guidelines, what we're all really after is always emotionally based; we want to *feel* good. In fact, why does anyone want wealth and abundance? For their own happiness, right? They think it will free them up so that they can be happier. Why would anyone want a new love life? Again, to be happier. Why would anyone want more friends, improved health, a new career, or creative fulfillment? The reason for all these things is more happiness.

In a sense, anything specific that you might be after in your life is actually a stepping-stone to more happiness. In other words, any desire that is not happiness-based is a *cursed how* designed to bring about happiness! Still, as the fun-loving otters of the Universe and as *matter manipulators* by birth, it's our prerogative to arrange the material stage of our lives as we please. After all, as I tell my audiences, matter is pure spirit, only more so! Remember, it's all God, and so it's all good. There's no harm in being materialistic as long as it is not *all* you're about and as long as being so isn't making you unhappy at present.

We live on the plane of manifestation in an adventure of the grandest sort. We are natural-born creators, and shaping, accumulating, and forging matter is one of our specialties. So there's room in all our lives to exercise these abilities, willfully, especially in the pursuit of even more happiness. In large part, it's one of the very reasons we are even here—to learn of our divinity and power. However, if we try too hard, insisting on change (or else!), hinging our happiness on every manifestation, and ignoring the greatness of all that already is and who we already are, we begin stressing ourselves out and tying the hands of the Universe.

An alternative to visualizing details, circumstances, and events is to spend those five or ten minutes simply feeling happy and joyful, not just for the happiness it will precipitate during the exercise but also because the Universe knows how to bring these feelings back to you on this plane of manifestation. And part of the logistics for making you as happy in your waking life as you are when you visualize is to literally begin changing your life, *physically speaking*, into one that will yield more happiness.

A NOTE FROM THE UNIVERSE

Happiness, dear heart, is what greases the wheels of life. It's also what opens the floodgates, marshals the forces, commands the elements, raises the sun, aligns the stars, beats your heart, heals what hurts, turns the page, makes new friends, finds true love, calls the shots, waves the wand, connects the dots, feeds your mind, frees your soul, rocks the world, and pays compound interest.

Yeah, so easy to forget.

Wild on,
The Universe

❊ TIME OUT ❊

The Magic of Thinking and Feeling Happy

When you express positive emotions and they vibrate out onto the plane of manifestation (as thoughts "trying" to become things), how does the Universe respond? It can't return to you a box of joy or a thing of gratitude. What does it do? It *physically* rearranges the players and circumstances of your life in such a way that they bring about exactly what you were feeling when you first put it out there in thought! This is *how* our *thoughts become things*! Even if it's a new car you want, it doesn't get plucked from thin air! Instead, circumstances are crafted that will put you on the right path (as you take action), in the right place, at the right time, with the right ideas, with enough money or whatever, to become the owner of your new car, just as you imagine it.

This ultimately means that you don't have to micromanage your thoughts to receive all the *things* you want in your life. If you put happiness out there—just pure happiness—it implies your overall well-being on all levels. When happiness is your mental focus and you take action on it (the second prerequisite for all change), your *entire* life, on all fronts, will be powerfully and positively affected, because feeling happiness *implies* you're going to have friends, feel well, possess sufficient funds, and do a host of other things that don't even need to be specifically thought of in advance to happen—ever!

❊   ❊   ❊

Mix it Up

Another way of gaining clarity of focus when you want to change many areas of your life is to come up with a plan. For example, on Mondays you visualize relationships, Tuesdays, creative fulfilling work, Wednesdays, abundance, and so on. Again, there are no rules!

Go BIG Picture

Finally, you could visualize a future scenario of your new, rocking life by creating a scene that implies that great change has already swept through many areas of your life. For example, you and your new (or renewed) love interest are traveling in first class to Hawaii for a holiday to celebrate a milestone being reached in your life (hypothetically, a new career, the sale of your company, your child's achievements, and so on). And in the first-class cabin, in each of its comfy sleeper seats, are four or five of your dearest friends and family members who are traveling with you to join the celebration. You're all laughing, proposing toasts, taking pictures, and recounting the dragons you've slain and the chasms you've crossed to earn this celebration. You're also excited because upon your arrival in Hawaii you'll be greeted not only by friends bearing leis but also your new realtor, who has listings to share with you for a possible vacation home, as well as the head of your charitable foundation, who has compelling reasons to open a branch on Oahu.

Outlandish? Yes! Materialistic? It's just an option! Realistic? Happens every day!

This scenario implies that you have found (or refound) the love of your life, you're healthy enough to jet set, you have friends galore and financial abundance, and you're creatively fulfilled, growing, and becoming even more of the person of your dreams than you were before. And this scene you imagine only needs to last a few minutes to capture it all! The following day, create a similar scenario with similar implications.

Lists for Love

On a number of occasions, women have asked for help with visualizing romantic love in their lives. Usually, they've made a list of their dream guy's qualities, but then "something" happens. I've heard many times, "Sure enough, I got every single quality on my list—but he was married! I forgot to write down that he should be single!" When I hear this, it's as if they really believe it was their oversight for not clarifying with the Universe that they wanted somebody who was single. We *do* need to be as clear as possible, but the Universe already knows you and what you're after. It isn't going to play a funny trick on you and retort, "Ha, ha, you should have told me 'single.' You didn't tell me. How could I have known?"

When such unexpected manifestations appear, there's a host of possible reasons, none of which are the Universe splitting hairs. One could be that the manifestation process was still in full progress and you hadn't yet met the person who was on the way. You only thought he (the married one) was your manifestation, yet in thinking this, you may well have blocked who you were otherwise about to meet! Other reasons could be due to limiting beliefs, such as "all the good guys are taken" (so you meet a taken one) or perhaps some conflicting beliefs about new relationships and/or marriage.

We *do* need to be as clear as possible, but the Universe already knows you and what you're after.

Having said that, I'll add that you can't put down too many details when making a list of desired end results. It's for your own edification, far more than the Universe's. This goes back to knowing what *you want*. The clearer we are in terms of what we want, the clearer the response from life's magic. The point I'm making is that should you forget to put down some detail about the life or love of your dreams, you needn't fret that you might unintentionally sabotage yourself for the omission. What's most important is that you go back to happiness as your ultimate desired end result, implying that all else is well.

A favorite quote of mine from the Bible is "For your Father knoweth what things ye have need of, before ye ask him" (Matthew 6, King James). And it's no wonder since your greater self extends to include the entire Universe! The Universe knows exactly what will make you happy. Visualization or mantras or whatever you use to conjure up thoughts are just tools for leveraging the Universe and engaging the magic so that you can align your thinking, get clear with your desires, start from where you are, and take action.

Create and Use a Mantra

Another trick for focusing and intensifying your thoughts, and perhaps also for narrowing down a broad field of changes you want to manifest in your life, is coming up with a few words that capture all these changes, such as a mantra—a phrase or just words that you mentally or verbally repeat to yourself. For instance, when I returned from my foreign assignment in the Middle East and was living in Boston, I wanted to change almost everything about my life. So I came up with four keywords that summed up my priorities and repeated them to myself to the cadence of my steps while walking to and from work: "I am *happy, spiritual, international,* and *a million-aire*. . . I am a *happy, spiritual, international,* and *a millionaire.*"

I wanted to be *happy*—I could have stopped there, but as a "matter manipulator," I had preferences and wanted to be very clear! I wanted to be *spiritual,* never losing sight of my own divinity and the true cause of the circumstances that surround us in time and space. I wanted to be *international.* I had already lived overseas and done a lot of traveling, and I wanted more—lots more. Finally, just to be safe, I wanted to be a *millionaire.* Those four things covered everything that I was most concerned about. This little mantra would give me great comfort, just knowing that I had the clarity to name what was most important to me, and beyond clarity, I knew that my mantra was allowing me to be aggressive and go on the offence, conjuring up thoughts that matched what I was thinking and saying.

When I repeated this mantra walking to and from work, often simultaneously visualizing, I always added in (felt) the emotion of happiness (for the reasons already given—it's what we really want and *implies* that so much more is going well in our life). I *felt* what it would feel like to be happy, spiritual, international, *and* a millionaire. I would pump myself up with every step I took, saying those words again and again. Actually, thinking back, I *didn't* have a lot of images running through my head, but that's OK because images pale in importance to emotion. Emotions are where it's at, and creating a mantra can help you feel them.

How I Go on the Offensive in Thought (and Take Action) as a Writer

I'm often flattered to be asked what my daily process is when writing the *Notes from the Universe.* Here's what I do:

First, I visualize the feeling I'm after—the end result.

After having done this for years, I know now what it feels like when I think I've written a really excellent *Note*. I often pump my fist in the air, yelp a few "whoo-hoos," and declare something to the effect of, "*Oh my God! I love this job.* I can't believe I'm doing this. I get to laugh before anyone else," usually while I'm still laughing at whatever I just hammered out.

Being so familiar with this *emotional feeling* and knowing that it's *this feeling* of having written really well that I want (which implies that I *have* written well), I work the process backwards. I begin with the desired end result in mind. When I visualize, I imagine feeling this same joy, pumping my fists in the air and whooping, knowing that the only way I can experience this on the plane of manifestations, physically, *is if I write well*! This is what summons the magic! The creativity! The bright ideas! I then meet this magic and these ideas when I follow the next step.

Second, I start from where I am, taking action.

I start writing whatever comes to mind, *writing anything* if I have to. Sometimes it's gibberish, sometimes it's nonsense, and I rarely have any idea where it's going to go, but by taking action, *after* having programmed the end result with my emotional visualization, eventually—*and it usually takes an hour or longer*—I manifest the very feelings I first put out there, only this time it's for having written well.

This one-two approach is how to bring about *anything* in time and space.

A Note from the Universe

The odd thing about inspiration is that it usually comes after, not before, a new journey has started.

*So go on, break the ice! Put on that tutu, spin a whirly, clutch the sky,
and you'll have them quivering in their boots in no time at all.*

Or am I thinking of someone else?

Yippee ki-yay!
The Universe

How You Get Proactive Is Not as Important as That You Do!

I just said that I visualize daily to aid my writing. Is that in addition to my five or ten minutes? Yes, although my writing visualization usually lasts only about a minute. Remember, there are no rules; I only offer guidelines.

But let me back up to the five- or ten-minute visualization. Five or ten minutes is a maximum, not a minimum. If you want to visualize less, absolutely go for it. Brief visualizations (of at least a minute) are probably more beneficial and give you an easier way to stay fresh and avoid daydreaming than longer, more drawn-out visualizations. If it suits you, try visualizing for two or three minutes at a time, several times a day. Perhaps every time you do this, do it with your focus on a different subject. For example, going to work, you might visualize success at the office. Coming home, you might visualize a happy social life. When you're starting a new project, as I do daily with the *Notes from the Universe*, imagine and visualize that brief feeling of emotional satisfaction or euphoria that you're after.

And if you forget to visualize for a week or a month or two years, don't worry; just start fresh from wherever you are. Many people have never had a visualization program, yet they've made stunning successes of their lives. They just used their imagination instinctively and automatically. They kept moving toward their dream. They believed it was possible. You can too.

But you have an advantage. You now know *how* Muhammad Ali became the greatest boxer, how J. K. Rowling became a great storyteller, how Oprah Winfrey climbed the ladder to stellar success, to use well-known figures as examples. They were able to hold on to a vision of their desired end results and they did whatever they could, with what they had, from where they were, all of which becomes even easier for the person who understands the workings of the Universe and its magic. With that in mind, why *wouldn't* you visualize?

A NOTE FROM THE UNIVERSE

Well, well, well, look at you! Back on top of the world!
What a picture! How splendid! Hallelujah!

New friends to cavort with, wild critters sensing your confidence,
and children holding you in awe. Laughter ringing in your ears,
happy tears streaming down your face, and arms aching from
all those hugs. My goodness, if some of your old friends
could see you now, they'd faint.

You've been visualizing, haven't you?

Beaming for you,
The Universe

P.S. Funny, isn't it, how thinking about something all the time isn't
quite the same as visualizing for just a few minutes a day?

Working with Our Words

Let's move on to the fulcrum of our words and choosing them defensively and offensively. Our words are simply our thoughts with enough intensity built up over time that they've actually rolled off our tongues. Our actions, too, are no more than our thoughts with enough intensity built up that they've thrown us into motion. So talking about our words and actions is very simply more talk about our thoughts becoming things, yet with different footholds and different leverage points to give you more ideas and tools to work with.

Being on the Defense

To start this off, let me recount another *Note* that speaks to understanding. Understanding is indeed, as I said in *Infinite Possibilities*, the elixir of life. It summons confidence, clarity, and guidance. With it, we know how to think, what to say, and when to act, in spite of circumstances presently surrounding us.

A NOTE FROM THE UNIVERSE

What if suddenly, in a flash of fire and light, you got "it"?
And among other things, you suddenly understood, without a doubt,
the creative power of your word? Do you think you'd ever again utter, "It's
hard," "It's not working," "Something's wrong with me," or "I don't know"?

Nope, you wouldn't—not ever again.

You've got "it."
The Universe

Do *you* get it? It's not enough to know that the principle of *thoughts become things* and then to routinely lament with friends over the state of the world, for example, or bemoan that looking at food makes you gain weight. *Speaking negatively* still gives the Universe marching orders. Of course, there's a place—a teeny, tiny place—to convey thoughts of your predicament or circumstances to a therapist, coach, or best friend when you need to express how you're feeling, so those feelings can be allowed to move on and be replaced. Yet choose your listeners well because well-intended commiseration such as, "Ain't it awful?" "Life's not fair," and "Can you believe this?" still commands every element and all the forces of nature to perpetuate your situation through acts of serendipity and coincidence.

And on the plane of manifestation you *cannot* say things— anything—without influencing the circumstances you experience next. Negative statements such as, "Lo and behold, I met another guy who treated me like dirt," "Another person ripped me off," or "I met another liar," explicitly tell the Universe that *this* is the kind of world *you* live in, and it replies—*with circumstances and manifestations*—essentially saying, "Roger, got ya. More of the same coming right up!" We reap what we sow.

On the plane of manifestation you *cannot* say things— anything—without influencing the circumstances you will experience next.

Even self-deprecating humor should be abandoned, unless you're a paid comedian. It may be good for a momentary chuckle, but is it worth the price? How many times have you heard someone say, "I just had a senior moment"? Even though said in jest, it's still what the Universe is going to respond to if you say it enough times, because the more you say it the more *you'll* believe it!

I'm So Tired

My first big lesson with words came while I was dating my first girlfriend when I was in high school. I can remember dreading those quiet times when we'd both run out of things to say. I'd silently wonder if she really ran out of things to say, or if perhaps she was beginning to have a change of heart. My mind would race. "Did I say something stupid? Doesn't she like me anymore? Could this be the beginning of the end?" Being young, green, and in love, I didn't know what to do, so I'd just blabber on about anything.

At the same time that I had this new girlfriend, my uncle from the United Kingdom was visiting, and he had a phrase he'd often say; it was like his personal mantra. He'd say, "I'm so tired. I'm so *bloody* exhausted." Well, needing to fill up the silence and willing to talk about *anything* with my girlfriend, I began using my uncle's words without even realizing it. In those silent moments I'd say, "Wow. I'm really tired today. I'm so tired. Are you tired? *I'm* just exhausted!" I can assure you, this is no way to foster young love, because they're *not* just words. I actually "became" them and was always feeling exhausted!

Eventually my girlfriend asked, "Mike, why are you *always* so tired?" *And I couldn't answer her!* I had completely forgotten that I started saying I was tired just to fill up the silence, and had then continued saying it because *I was*!

Even though I wasn't using the phrase *thoughts become things* back then, I had already begun my journey into understanding the powers of thought and the mind. One day I wondered what would happen if I stopped saying I was so tired. Whoa! My sudden rejuvenation in the days that followed was shocking—almost scary! Scary because I began thinking about what might have happened had I not stopped declaring my exhaustion, or if I had begun saying other unhelpful things about myself that would have also become true!

I'll bet you believe that you, too, could make yourself tired, just as I did, simply by saying that you feel exhausted, again and again, day in and day out. Right? But what if tomorrow morning you woke up feeling like a "million bucks," like you were on top of the world, king or queen of your reality, bursting with enthusiasm and exuberance, aware that your thoughts became the things and events of your life? What if then, in spite of feeling so great, you said, "I'm tired. I'm so tired. I'm absolutely exhausted"? If you said it enough times, even though you weren't telling the truth, would you still succeed in making yourself tired? Yes, no doubt about it.

Let's make this even more challenging. Let's pretend that you keep up this ruse and that you *want* to become tired, even though you're not, but you're not allowed to read any more self-improvement or metaphysical books to remind you of the power of your words in the world around you. And let's further say that you refuse the help of family, friends, therapy, or coaching to help you "become exhausted." You're on your own. Do you think you'd still succeed in becoming tired? Yes, you'd be good at this!

So *do you see*? Do you see how *incredibly* easy it is to spark change in your life? Simply start by speaking about yourself as if you are already the person of your dreams, and about your life as if it were already how you've always dreamed it might be, as if you already "have it all"! Do you also see that what you say doesn't even have to be true at first? In fact, it won't be true; otherwise, you wouldn't want change! So start saying these types of things, *especially* when they're not yet your experience—*this is when you need to say them the most*! And do you see how you don't need more CDs or books (after this one, of course)? You don't need the help and support of others. And you don't have to figure out your phobias, unravel your past, or know who you were in the twelfth century! Of course, there's a place for books, friends, and therapy; what I'm saying, however, is that you're now capable and powerful enough to begin creating change in your life simply by using your thoughts and words wisely, in ways that serve you.

Going on the Offense

Choosing your words to spark change doesn't just work with your energy levels; *it works with everything*! Right now, you can start saying things like, "I've got all the time in the world," "I'm surrounded by wealth and abundance," "Everything I touch turns to gold," "I love public speaking," "I never get jet lag," "I always have exactly the right thing to say at the right time to the right person," "I'm always in the right place at the right time," "My life is so easy," "I know what I'm going to do today, tomorrow, and for the rest of my life," and "I have total clarity, total certainty." And, of course, there's my personal favorite, which I shared in *Manifesting Change*: "I'm so-o-o-o-o photogenic! I can't take a bad picture!"

More than once I've heard the following objection to what I've just told you: "Mike, I feel like I'm being dishonest if I say everything I touch turns to gold, when in reality I've got $50,000 of credit card debt!" To which I reply, "Which reality?"

We are unlimited beings of light for whom all things are possible. Presently, we live in a dream world—a world made up of our thoughts, a world in which we are nothing more than who we think and say we are, a world in which we get to choose our perspectives and the truths we focus upon, where anything can happen, and every day, all over the world, dreams *are* coming true! Isn't saying that you're broke, lonely, or ill a lie when you simultaneously see yourself as pure God? You may have dallied in poverty consciousness and are now temporarily experiencing a constriction in cash flow, but does that mean you are a "poor person"? You may be "poor" today, but that is not *who* you are, and it bears no indication of where you're headed. You are rich. You were born rich. And you will always be rich in a world that bends to your thoughts, words, and deeds.

Today's manifestations came from yesterday's thoughts, words, and actions. Tomorrow's manifestations will begin taking shape based on what we think, say, and do today. We are all mid-journey here in time and space; our lives are a work in progress, yet to pick any day of that journey and use it to define "who we are" is like reading a novel halfway through and then writing a book review on it.

Of course, I'm *not* suggesting that you tell everyone about this "reality" or how you now see yourself. Choose words that suit the company you're in. But among friends who get this stuff and to yourself, let your words reflect the celebration of creation that your life *is*.

A NOTE FROM THE UNIVERSE

Just curious: when was the last time you looked into a mirror and addressed yourself as "Gorgeous," "Magnificent," or "Sublime"?

It matters.

Here's looking at you, Gorgeous.
The Universe

Working with Our Deeds

The fulcrum of our actions is perhaps the most powerful resource. Watching how we behave not only tips us off to what we are truly *thinking*, thereby enabling us to correct our thoughts and behavior, but by deliberately acting out of step with our present circumstances, we also powerfully influence changing our circumstances, vis-à-vis the new thoughts those actions trigger.

Being on the Defense

Working defensively is the same as working with our thoughts and words. Simply pay attention to what you're doing. If each week when you go to the grocery store you're buying the cheapest, most generic products to save money, catch yourself. What are your actions saying to the Universe about your belief in the avalanches of abundance and resources that are now rushing toward you? Not much.

Are you holding yourself back in your relationships? Perhaps you don't want your heart broken again, so you're not offering it fully to your new partner. Are you doing the same at work, not being fully engaged? In these examples, you may as well shout to the Universe, "There may be hard times ahead!" and the Universe metaphorically responds, "Roger, got you loud and clear." Catch yourself, and then after holding your action up to the light of truth, change your thoughts and *your behavior* with an act of faith that implies success, strength, and confidence.

Going on the Offense

Going on the offense is different from the baby steps we've already talked about, though such baby steps are themselves powerful declarations of your intended success. Going on the offense, as I mean it here, however, is about either physically *preparing* for your dream to come true or acting as if it *already* has come true. Let's look at both.

Acting "As If": Preparing for Your Inevitable Success

The demonstration of *physically preparing* for your dream to arrive sends shock waves into the unseen, evidencing your own thoughts and implied new beliefs about your inevitable success. To help you understand what I mean when I say "physically prepare," let's hypothetically say that this evening you go shopping for new living room furniture. After you make the purchase, the salesperson informs you that your furniture will be delivered next Thursday at 3 o'clock in the afternoon. From this point forward, once you got home, what would you be doing in anticipation of its delivery? You'd begin *physically preparing* for its inevitable arrival. You'd be getting rid of the old stuff or moving it into another room. You might go shopping for some new pillows, maybe a new matching area rug, or even new lamps and curtains. You wouldn't go home from the furniture store, put your head between your hands and lament, "My gosh, what if it never shows up?"

> **The demonstration of *physically preparing* for your dream to arrive sends shock waves into the unseen, evidencing your own thoughts and implied new beliefs about your inevitable success.**

The same is true when you place your order with the Universe. It *has* to show up. It always shows up when you do your part, one component of which can be *physically preparing* for its arrival!

Now let's pretend that your big dream today is to own a new set of living room furniture, but you can't afford it with your present budget. What do you do? *Buy the pillows!* In addition to visualizing, choosing your words wisely, and taking baby steps in the direction of getting new furniture, you can also regularly and frequently prepare the way for its inevitable arrival. And by obvious extension, also begin physically preparing for the inevitable changes that are coming to every area of your life that you now dreaming of changing.

Make It a Family Affair

A woman wrote to me shortly after the audio program of *Infinite Possibilities* was released, very excited by my talk on the subject of *acting* with faith. She was already familiar with metaphysical concepts in general, but during the time she was listening to the "acts of faith" section of my audio program, she also heard about an upcoming basketball free-throw competition to be sponsored by a local chain of bars, in which contestants had one attempt to make a basket from across the court. The contestant who succeeded would win *$1 million*. She was inspired!

Summoning her extended family, she carefully instructed each of them on how to *physically prepare* for the celebration party she envisioned they would have once her athletic brother made the basket and won the money! Obviously, her brother had to enroll in the contest. Another family member was given the responsibility of dealing with the press, another was in charge of invitations, another was in charge of calling hotels with ballrooms to decide where the party would be held, someone had to price out the entertainment, and so on. Of course, I wouldn't be telling you this story had he not made the winning shot. They had their party!

I have friend who's a karate champion who said to me, "I've done this 'acting as if' my whole life." He's one of those people who doesn't intellectually know much about the Universe or Its magic but who naturally engages it. He has a wall full of trophies from karate tournaments he's entered and won. He explained,

"Whenever I have a new tournament coming up, I go to my trophy shelves before the tournament begins, and I decide where the new one will go. I then move my other trophies around to make a place for it in advance." He prepares the way.

Other perhaps mundane but equally powerful examples of acting as if in a preparatory sense include going to school, getting licenses, printing business cards, doing research, or buying a social calendar to manage your exciting life!

A NOTE FROM THE UNIVERSE

Straight from the fabled Akashic Records (shhhhhh):

Time and Space is where you chase things you pretend you don't have—love, friends, and abundance—while worrying about things you pretend you do have—problems, challenges, and issues—until one day you happen to notice the prophetic powers of pretending.

In case that helps any.

Tallyho!
The Universe

Acting As If Your Dream Has Already Come to Pass

You can also playfully act as if you are already living in a world where your dream or dreams has come true. If you're not well, act as if you're healthy. If you're broke, act as if you're wealthy. If you're lonely, act as if you have friends. If you have a lot of debt, as I suggested in *Infinite Possibilities*, don't ever pay the minimum allowed on your monthly statement; pay more, even if you only round up to the next dollar, as if you already have more money (you're also reducing your principle). People who pay the minimum are those who believe that their resources are limited and doubts that abundance is on its way, whereas by paying just a bit more, even if only cents, this act implies that they *do* have the financial discretion and freedom that they now dream of having—and this act (when combined with all else I'm sharing) literally summons circumstances that will manifest the resources that will avail them of such discretion and freedom.

Tipping is another way you can act as if you've already achieved your dreams. Don't ever just tip the standard 15 percent. Always tip more. Think about it: what's the real cost of tipping a little more? A couple of extra dollars, in most cases! Give to charities, if only a few dollars, give to family or anonymously to strangers, or help causes that are meaningful to you. Overtipping and giving aren't going to make you any less abundant. To the contrary, they offer a fulcrum from which you can leverage life's magic, as doing so helps *you* believe in the abundant world in which you really do live: a *spiritual* world. And in *this* world, spending more than the minimum, tipping, and gifting imply that you are provided for, that you have means and choices, and that you've played the money game well—and so it shall be.

Of course, acts of faith aren't limited to spending money. And if you simply don't have any money or you're deep in debt, going further into debt as an act of faith is not your ticket. Understanding your power also means understanding your responsibilities, and to understand both, we need to honestly look at the progress we've made, or haven't made, and not add salt to our wounds. If you're presently in debt, clearly the "spending money to make money" concept needs a rest, during which you can playfully act the part of millionaire in many other ways.

One of my acts of faith eleven years ago, when I had my back to the wall financially and didn't know how I'd restart my life, was shopping regularly at a boating supply store. As a boy, I grew up on the water and we always had a boat. As an act of faith that my fortunes had turned, I'd pretend that I already had a boat! You don't walk into a boating supply store unless you're a boat owner, so to me this implied that my "ship" (in this case, boat) had come in and that I was financially well off. I'd even go out of my way on Saturdays just to visit this store, hang around for an hour or so, buy some keychain floats or cold drink holders, and return home. I wouldn't make any deviations or run any errands on the way there or back because I wanted it to be a crystal-clear act of faith that I was a person who owned a boat, which implied that my finances were rocking.

Reverse Worrying

On my first visit to London during my first world tour, I was really nervous about speaking to a British audience. I had just flown across the Atlantic and was still new to speaking, and in two days, I was going to talk for four hours to an audience of forty people who had each paid upwards of $200 for the "privilege." I was really scared—afraid I'd ramble, misspeak, lose my train of thought, or otherwise disappoint the audience. The day before my event, I sequestered myself in my hotel room, paced, rehearsed, made outlines, and went over my material again and again until I was a nervous wreck. I actually wondered if my intense pacing would wear the carpet to any noticeable degree. Of course, I was very aware that *thoughts become things* and that worrying like that and rehearsing excessively (*acting as if I could fail*) was not the right message to send to the Universe and life's magic!

I desperately thought, "I need to counter this!" because it seemed impossible to stop myself from worrying (similar to the "simultaneously starting a new train running" approach that I spoke of earlier). So I physically wrote a list of all the reasons why my event "*had been*" so wildly successful (as if it had already happened in the past and I was remembering it, explaining its success).

As soon as I began making this list, I started to feel better, because this act of faith implied that the event had already gone well and it made me realize that there were lots of reasons that it might do so! Reasons that, until I wrote my list, were the furthest from my mind. All of a sudden I had to *justify* my wild success, whereas, before this act, it seemed that all I could think of were reasons why it might be a disaster. I wrote down the obvious, such as, "I'm prepared. I've already given this talk twice." And then I had to struggle to come up with more, *causing* me to think things I had never thought before. One of my reasons, which tickled me pink and I *still* use, is that "I must be a natural-born speaker!"

I came up with other reasons too: The audience wanted me to do well. I had a great sleep the night before. The hotel staff where my event was held was awesome. I had no problems or issues with the setup in the morning. And so on. I made the list as long as I could, really letting my imagination loose, in an exercise I now refer to as "reverse worrying."

Later that same day I reviewed my list and was suddenly astounded when I thought of one more reason for my wild success that I had completely forgotten to include—the best reason of all: I live in a magical, loving Universe and I'm surrounded by life's magic! *The very thing that I was in London to talk about!* I slapped my head with a big "duh," and yet it felt absolutely fabulous to suddenly remember that I wasn't alone, that the Universe was conspiring on my behalf, that I had done all I could, with what I had, from where I was, and that the Universe would be doing the exact same thing in return.

Later that same day I reviewed my list and was suddenly astounded when I thought of one more reason for my wild success that I had completely forgotten to include— the best reason of all: I live in a magical, loving Universe and I'm surrounded by life's magic!

I imagined the Universe feeding me my lines, holding my hand, and helping me to address exactly what my audience most needed to hear and to be the best I could be with all the support I could ever want or need. Now, I'm not the sort who likes to brag . . . but the next day, at the end of my four-hour lecture, the forty or so in attendance gave me a mini standing ovation.

Give It to Yourself

Who said this has to be all work?

Just as baby steps themselves are acts of faith and powerful declarations of your intended success, so is enjoying who you already are and all you already have. If you allow yourself to appreciate, indulge, splurge, and celebrate today, your focus automatically includes all the good you've already manifested. You might not be able to buy the $1,000 suit yet, but perhaps you can buy the $500 suit, and you can begin enjoying it immediately. You can probably already afford the cool cell phone too—or the digital camera, a magazine subscription, or a new pair of shoes. And this isn't just about money. Take time off to do *nothing*, have friends over for tea, enjoy a nearby park or beach, reread your favorite book, stretch your limbs and go for a sunrise walk, watch the sunset, rearrange the furniture throughout your home, plant some flowers, watch movies all night, enjoy a long drive somewhere new—give these to yourself!

Like begets like and *thoughts become things*. Go on, give it to yourself, and enjoy what you already have. Such physical displays are not only fun but they're also powerful communications to the Universe and the magic that confirm you're on your way— a communication, which on the plane of manifestation, summons more of the same.

A NOTE FROM THE UNIVERSE

The secret to living the life of your dreams . . .

is to start living the life of your dreams at once,
to any degree that you possibly can.

I got you, babe.
The Universe

Gratitude

There's one last point I like sharing whenever I write about using the fulcrums of our thoughts, words, and deeds: gratitude. It's powerful, and here's why.

When you express gratitude or say "Thank you" to the Universe or your greater self, what you're actually saying is synonymous with "I have received." This is true whether you give thanks for what you already have or when you give thanks for what you desire *as if you already have it*—health, friends, love, and abundance. This is superpowerful! You're going beyond the end result; you're putting out gratitude to the Universe. And the only way the Universe can manifest that *emotion* back to you—that gratitude—is to manage circumstances, people, and players in your life that will yield the gratitude you first sent out.

Knowing this helps us be careful about our lists of desires. If you express your desires in terms of "I want, I want," you're also implying and stating to the Universe, "I don't have, I don't have." Not what you want to perpetuate! So when you're expressing your desires for change, the best way to do so is through expressions of gratitude—thanking the Universe *in advance* for the things that are on your wish list as if you already have them, while at the same time appreciating what you presently have. This works not because the Universe is passing judgment, waiting to see if you were thankful for the last lot of goodies it sent you before it gives you more, but because you live on an unjudging plane of manifestation, and whatever you put out there must come back—and if it's gratitude for having received, then you must receive in order for that gratitude to later manifest.

When You Need This the Most

Some of the suggestions I've offered in this chapter and in earlier ones may well seem a bit airy-fairy, particularly if you're facing dire circumstances. Perhaps your heart has just been broken, you've been diagnosed with a disease, or you've filed for bankruptcy protection, and then I come along and say, "Hey, just tell little 'lies' and pretend your life's OK." Unfortunately, the grinding emotional pains brought about by *physical circumstances* lead us to think that we must get very "real," and therefore very physical, to alleviate the pain. This is the degree of hold that the illusions defined by time, space, and matter have over us, making the simplicity of all I've suggested so far seem like suspicious-sounding "woo-woo" psychobabble. Unfortunately, again, this suspicion causes those who need these ideas the most to shrug them off.

I have a suggestion for both the skeptics and those now facing personal crises, to whom my ideas might seem insufficient: *play both ends to the middle.* In other words, by all means continue with your enrollment in the "school of hard knocks," worrying, plotting, showing up early, and staying late, *but for a change*, also try moonlighting with small, daily experiments in thoughts, words, and deeds. Because of your inborn inclination to succeed, any "harm" done by the old-school approaches (which tend to imply that we are helpless) will be more than offset with even the smallest doses of regularly practiced "woo-woo-isms."

Adapt These Ideas to Your Unique Life

Just as you'll do with visualizing, experiment and find techniques for using your thoughts, words, and deeds that are comfortable for you. You might be surprised where it leads you.

Years ago in the 1990s, when I first discovered Microsoft Outlook software for organizing contacts, calendars, email, and so forth, I discovered that you could set yourself reminders for important dates and times, like birthdays, doctor's appointments, or business meetings. After I became familiar with its suggested uses, I realized that I could also use it remind myself of other things at an appointed time every day, like, "You're dreaming, Mike! Time and space are illusions, and you have but to think new thoughts to experience new things!" "You are an unlimited being of light, for whom all things are possible!" and many more. I had a dozen "appointments" scheduled every week that were really just positive affirmations or truths that were designed to snap me back into an awareness of my power and life's magic.

Even after months of receiving these same daily "appointment" reminders, I'd still be surprised every time my computer "announced" a new one. Then it occurred to me: "Hey, wouldn't it be even cooler if I got an email every day with messages like these, sent from someone else so that I wouldn't know the punch line or affirmation in advance?" And so began the "Monday Morning Motivators," which eventually turned into the daily *Notes from the Universe*.

Those are just two electronic examples of how I was able to align my thinking with the life of my dreams. You could also experiment with using images and pictures in scrapbooks and vision boards and posting notes around your house. Images, incidentally, are particularly powerful because they automatically take you to the end result, completely bypassing the *cursed hows*. After all, you don't put a picture in your scrapbook of yourself hanging out at singles bars or looking for a new job! Instead, the images are always of the *end results* you're after.

Find what works for you and fits your schedule, and you'll not only make it easy on yourself but also be much more likely to stick with it.

Your New J-O-B

Your thoughts, your words, and your deeds are your only fulcrums for leveraging the Universe and engaging the magic. Just as you wouldn't bathe only once and then never again, neither would you dabble with creating permanent change part time. The reason you bathe regularly is because it works. The same is true of working with your thoughts, words, and deeds—defensively, by paying attention to all you think, say, and do, and then, in the simplest of ways, vigilantly going on the offense. Wanting change means thinking, speaking, and behaving in ways that we've never thought, spoken, or behaved before, consistently. You can do this; you've already been doing it, although unintentionally, as the years of your life have rolled by, and with practice, it becomes even easier to do more frequently and with intent.

> **Your thoughts, your words, and your deeds are your only fulcrums for leveraging the Universe and engaging the magic.**

Summary Points

* Our thoughts, words, and deeds are our only points of contact with the Universe and life's magic.
* Being on the defense with our thoughts, words, and deeds means vigilantly being aware of those that do not serve us and changing them to the best of our ability.
* When you're aboard a "runaway train of fear," let it run. But simultaneously start a new train running, with happier, more positive thoughts.
* Visualizing is one of the most effective uses of your time to spark change.
* Your words and your deeds are simply your thoughts with enough intensity that they've either rolled off your tongue or thrown you into action. Use them to find out what you're really thinking and to begin sparking new thoughts.
* The emotional energy of happiness literally rearranges the *material* aspects of your life—predisposing you to circumstances that will bring about even more happiness.

- The secret to living the life of your dreams is to start living them today, to any degree you can.
- There's no harm done playing both ends to the middle. In other words, continue with your old-school rituals for creating change while mixing in new-school approaches.
- Gratitude felt for what you have expands what you already have. Gratitude felt for what you want to receive, expressed as if you've already received it, hastens its arrival.

SUGGESTED EXERCISES

Going on the Offensive in Thought

Write a brief script for a scenario that you could visualize, which can be a starting point for a five- to ten-minute (maximum) visualization. Let there be a number of elements included that imply success and happiness. For example:

> *"I will take my new car* (be specific), *with its new-car feel and new-car smell, to pick up the children from school. I'll see the world around me from the vantage point of the driver's seat, cruising down familiar streets, watching the world watch me through the car's windows. I'll be singing and giddily bopping to my favorite Elton John CD, and friends and strangers will be giving me admiring glances as I glide by. At school, my kids will be beaming over the happy day they had, and I'll receive and hear compliments from other parents on my new clothes and overall appearance* (again, remember to be specific). *From school, I'll take us house hunting for our new home that will have lots of privacy and a large yard. While viewing a really cool home, my cell phone will ring its funky ring, and it*

will be a call from my agent, who's presently in New York shop-ping my latest manuscript. Just hearing her excited voice is enough to get me excited, and then she tells me . . ."

When your script is complete with its own ending, visualize it, once a day, until it gets boring, and then create a new script to visualize.

Going on the Offensive in Word

Create a palette for future use by making a list of things you can say about yourself, as if you are already the person living the life of your dreams. For example:

* "I am (surrounded by friends and laughter, always in the right place at the right time, happier than I've ever been before, a magnet to opportunity, for example)."
* "I love (how easy my life is, where I live, my amazing home, the person I have become, that my life experience and knowledge give me wisdom and peace, for example)."

Make these lists long, and keep in mind that they aren't phrases to recite once and then forget. Ideally they'll become part of your daily speech, naturally evolving to become more compre-hensive and reflective of your ever-evolving preferences and manifestations.

Going on the Offensive in Deed

List small acts of faith you can now perform in the coming days, weeks, and months, both to prepare for the inevitable arrival of your dreams' manifestations and as if your dreams have already come true. Later, of course, do them! Perhaps assign yourself one per day.

Do It Yourself

This chapter hints at many more things you can do to create your own custom-made exercises, like in the sections "Reverse Worrying" and "Gratitude." I suggest rereading those parts of this chapter and then putting pen to paper.

5

STEP FIVE:

ALIGN YOUR BELIEFS

Which do you think are more powerful: thoughts or beliefs? This is a loaded question, of course.

I hear from the occasional audience member, "Aren't our beliefs more important than the principle of *thoughts become things*?" Yes and no. The *reason* our beliefs are indeed almighty is because our *thoughts become things*. Our beliefs allow, enable, and encourage us to think within their boundaries. For example, Roger Federer wins professional tennis tournaments because he allows himself to actually think about winning tennis tournaments (undoubtedly *a lot*), and this is because he *first* believes that winning is a reasonable option. His thoughts make it happen, but his beliefs allow him to think those thoughts.

Our beliefs can also disallow us, or prevent us, from thinking beyond their scope when we believe something is "unlikely" or "impossible." And without such thoughts being entertained, there can be no corresponding manifestation. For example, when was the last time you *thought* about winning a professional tennis tournament? Too easy? Then when was the last time you even thought about living the life of your wildest dreams? Of course, baby steps and taking action are vital, but even here you will be shut down before you begin if your beliefs aren't supportive.

Obviously, the key to rather effortlessly thinking thoughts that serve us and blasting forward is to get our beliefs in order. Easy enough, right? Except that our beliefs are usually invisible. So when it comes to discerning which of yours are "helpful" and which may be "hurtful," the course of action I propose is *not* to go scavenging for what can't be seen but to more simply *align* yourself with your dreams through a few simple exercises so that you *automatically* install supporting, reflective beliefs while *automatically* shedding unhelpful beliefs.

A NOTE FROM THE UNIVERSE

Quantum Physics 101:

The present is defined by a confluence of your thoughts, guided and restricted by your beliefs. The future is what you experience when your beliefs change. Time measures how much energy or effort you require to change your thoughts, or the degree of conflict between old and new beliefs. And space shows exactly what you're now thinking about.

And therein you see that the one universal, immovable, unifying equation that sums up all things physical and metaphysical is Thoughts Become Things, *which is all you really need to know.*

TBT,
The Universe

P.S. Of course time travel is possible. You're doing it now.

Putting the Cart before the Horse: Jumping to Conclusions

People do recognize that beliefs are almighty, but they often, unfortunately, then draw the conclusion that in order to effect change in their life, they must first change their beliefs, which is based on the shaky premise that if they *don't* already have what they want—for instance, wealth and abundance or friends and laughter—then it must be due to some self-sabotaging, invisible, limiting belief that they *do* possess, which may not be true at all.

This is a scary approach because on the plane of manifestation, whatever we focus on long enough, followed up with action, we either find or manifest! That's the way things work in time and space. It ultimately works for living in abundance, if that's where you place your energy, *and it ultimately works for finding out what's wrong with you*, if that's where you place your energy, even if there was nothing wrong with you to begin with! Maybe limiting beliefs weren't the culprit; however, if people are continually walking around saying to themselves and others things like, "I must not believe I'm worthy," or "I don't know what it is, but I seem to be getting in my own way with limited thinking," this shall then become their reality!

We either find or manifest everything in our lives, including the circumstances that perpetuate what we're focusing on, just as I did with my "I'm so tired" mantra, even though when I started saying it, it wasn't true.

There could be many other reasons that something is not yet in your life—in spite of how long you've wanted it—none of which may be linked to invisible, limiting beliefs. Perhaps it's been a matter of your priorities or a matter of wanting to organize your life in a certain way before taking action in new directions, or perhaps it was simply not *understanding* how powerful and deserving you already are. Yet the moment you jump to the conclusion that there must be something wrong with you or that you must have invisible limiting beliefs holding you back, then BAM! It becomes your reality! The cart is now firmly in front of the horse, and such conclusions become your beliefs, creating thoughts, influencing your behavior, and ultimately *becoming an issue that will indeed hold you back*, without your ever uncovering the true reason(s) that perhaps kept you from what you wanted.

Making things even more complicated, those who believe they must first find this presumed-to-exist invisible limiting belief to create change further believe that they must then pull that sucker out by its roots and cast it into oblivion in order to make progress. Yet what often happens, whether or not the belief even existed to begin with, is that once people claim it, instead of throwing it away, they carry it around with them as if it were a little baby, telling everyone about their issue: "This is what happened to me when I was four years old; this is what happened to me when I was in high school and my heart was broken; this is what happened to me the first time I got a job" and so forth. They use this invisible, limiting belief (its prior validity or lack thereof is irrelevant) as a crutch or justification to explain why they aren't further along in life, all while either establishing or reinforcing the new belief that they really do have a problem!

You Don't Have to Know How You Got Where You Are Today

There are other ways to create change in your life—ways that include working with your beliefs without drawing the conclusion that there's something wrong with you. Just as *where* you are is not *who* you are, neither do you have to explain what brought you to this day in order to purposefully and deliberately blast forward.

The premise that I live by and that works for me, and that I've seen work for countless others, begins with realizing that the only thing separating you today from living the life of your dreams tomorrow are the thoughts you think between now and then—remembering that your thoughts include your words and your actions. Your destination and the steps you take toward it are all you have to focus on. In fact, as you'll see in this chapter, when you vigilantly work on your thoughts defensively and offensively, your beliefs will automatically align to serve you. And *if* you do have any invisible, limiting beliefs that were holding you back, they'll no longer make sense in light of your new thoughts, words, and deeds and eventually lose their hold over your wandering mind and completely vanish, *whether or not you even became aware of what they were.*

A NOTE FROM THE UNIVERSE

While I would actually LOVE to help every living soul on the planet remember who they were in prior lives, why the pyramids were really built, and how their past beliefs shaped present manifestations, I'd infinitely prefer to help them bust a move here and now, learn some new tricks, and live their dreams, which, incidentally, is the only reason anyone ever chooses to come back.

Let's do this.
The Universe

P.S. Suffice it to say, Your Highness, you've always been crazy-sexy-cool.

My "Train Wreck" Revisited

When it had seemed that my life had completely become unglued during my so-called train wreck, while I neither knew (or cared to know) what was wrong with me, nor could I explain the seeming "mess" I had created, I could still, nevertheless, explain how life worked, and how to incite change and live deliberately. *Thoughts become things!* Yet to more practically state it, the following two steps reiterate and condense all I've shared so far in this book, regarding the base fundamentals of how to leverage the universe and engage life's magic:

The Two Steps Necessary for Manifesting All Life Changes:

1. Define what you want in terms of its end result—the "finished product."

2. Take unending baby steps toward it.

Had I not understood the above and thought I needed to figure out what was "wrong" with me in order to move forward, I may have sought professional help. My life, at that moment, wasn't a pretty picture: I was unemployed, had no relationship, and was clueless as to where I was headed. I felt like I had nothing to look forward to. A classic midlife crisis, *if* I wanted to view it that way. But I truly believe that had I gone that route, looking for what was wrong with me, I would have found stuff—oh yes, no surprise, *lots* of stuff—and I further believe I'd still be working on fixing it all! I'd never have given myself permission to write and speak about life, which subsequently made possible all that I enjoy today. The so-called discovery (or better yet, *manifestation*) of one debilitating belief after another that would likely have followed such a choice (to figure out what was wrong with me), and each would have required an army of professionals to help me undo them. I also would have uncovered plenty of valid reasons to justify not being further along in my life—which, of course, would have been very comforting. Big whoop!

Looking back today I can see that the train of my life never derailed; it simply *changed tracks!* It's just that I was so close to the seeming commotion and so inclined, as we naturally are in these primitive times, to jump to conclusions—thinking that I was bad, broken, and in need of repair, that it was hard for me to imagine any other possible conclusion at the time other than "train wreck"!

> **I didn't need to figure out my past or unravel my beliefs in order to blast forward—and neither do you. *You just need to move forward*, and then the right beliefs will assemble themselves around you quickly enough.**

With the benefit of hindsight, however, I can now see that before the "commotion," I wrote about life, dreams, and happiness for our T-shirt business while dreaming of one day reaching more people. After the "commotion," and to this very day, I *still* write about life, dreams, and happiness, but now I reach more people— *tens of millions more* if you count those who have read or watched *The Secret*. The career momentum, which seemed to have completely vanished, was actually there all along! My career wasn't over; it was just in the process of *magically* ramping up to warp speed, which necessitated the "train" of my life *changing tracks!*

I didn't need to figure out my past or unravel my beliefs in order to blast forward—and neither do you. *You just need to move forward*, and then the right beliefs will assemble themselves around you quickly enough.

✳ TIME OUT ✳

Professional Help

Of course, innumerable people have benefited greatly from receiving professional life guidance, whether from doctors, therapists, coaches, counselors, or skilled friends, and I don't want to deter you from choosing that course if it makes sense and feels right.

One of the first things professionals will make clear is that their service is of a temporary and supportive nature, designed to liberate you and enrich *the rest of your life*. It's about freeing yourself from the past, enjoying the present, and deliberately creating your future.

Again, play both ends to the middle. Very likely, your guides will advise the same. While following the tried-and-true old-school methods for invoking change that they may share with you, you can mix in a bit of visualizing, playful pretending, acting "as if," and taking lots of baby steps. Remind yourself about the truth behind life's mechanics. *Thoughts become things*. Use your time with them to focus on your strengths, your magnificence, your divinity, your power, and the infinite possibilities that always exist for all of us to live happier, more fulfilling lives, no matter where we've been so far.

✳ ✳ ✳

Align Your Beliefs with the Life of Your Dreams

If all that stands between your life today and living the life of your dreams tomorrow are the thoughts you think between now and that future, then let's reverse engineer this. I first talked about reverse engineering in *Infinite Possibilities* when I suggested using our actions to *change* our beliefs. Doing this requires two simple steps:

1. Identify the beliefs that would serve you.

2. Install those beliefs by acting as if they're already yours.

By working backwards from our *desired* beliefs and then behaving as if they're ours, they will actually *become* ours, while simultaneously bulldozing whatever limiting beliefs we may have had.

Identify the Beliefs That Serve You

With your dream in mind, list the beliefs that would obviously and logically be helpful to have. *You don't have to claim that they're now yours*—just name them. This is so much easier than fishing around for invisible limiting beliefs that you may *or may not* have. Just identify the beliefs that you'd like to be yours. In addition to serving as the first step for installing new beliefs, this exercise will leave you with a sense of your potential and buoy you with optimism, as it hints of future successes without focusing on what "might be" wrong with you.

Beliefs That Would Support Living in Abundance

I could have picked any hypothetical example to illustrate the belief systems that would support a life of abundance, like finding abundant relationships, health, or friendships, but in my experience, financial abundance is what most people want to draw into their lives first. Here, I'll enumerate a list of the beliefs that would likely be part of your constitution if you have *already* accumulated financial abundance. If you'd like change elsewhere in your life, write a constitution similar in structure to the one below but with beliefs that would likely be yours if you had *already* achieved the aspect of change you envision. In the case of financial abundance:

- *I'm worthy.* I can't count how many people have come to me and said something like, "I don't have wealth and abundance, and I think it must be because I don't believe I'm worthy. My parents didn't think they were worthy, and now I don't think I'm worthy." Maybe that's true—*but maybe it's not.* Either way, don't claim it for yourself because then you own it, perpetuate it, and experience it. *Do* say that you're worthy. Spell it out in words that have meaning to you. You are worthy—own it.
- *I'm deserving.* And not just because you've perhaps worked hard, endured lack, and suffered hardships but also because you're a child of the Universe: you're caring, you're loving, and, as Khalil Gibran wrote in *The Prophet*, because you're obviously worthy to "receive your days," from God, the Universe, or Divine Intelligence, surely you must see you're worthy of all else.
- *There's enough for everyone.* You live in a dream world made of illusions—illusions that you perpetuate with your thoughts. It's only our limited physical senses that tell us there's scarcity, and that view is based on the presumption that time and space are bedrock reality, which takes us back to eating the forbidden fruit. There is enough for everyone in this Garden of Eden we call home, this heaven on earth, this oasis amongst the stars, where literally, as Neale Donald

Walsch so aptly pointed out, money does in fact grow on trees![1] Not only is there enough for everyone but you having yours doesn't stop others from having theirs. You can drop the senseless guilt—really, you can.

* *Having more wealth and abundance will enable me to help more people.* Of course, you can help and give and share and change the world without a penny to your name, but certainly there's nothing wrong with the belief that you can reach more people by having wealth and abundance. Finally, this casts wealth and abundance in a favorable light, a spiritual one, and it'll certainly work to negate the old religious dogmas that cast wealth and abundance in a dark, sinister, and unspiritual light.

* *My thoughts become the things and events of my life.* Start factoring in your spiritual insights—they are, after all, supremely relevant! You have dominion over all things. You're an eternal being of light for whom the Universe and life's magic conspires.

* *Amassing wealth is easy. Thoughts become things,* and it's no more difficult to playfully imagine a million dollars than it is to imagine one dollar. Give yourself permission to think big.

* *God wants me to be rich.* Not to turn the equation of happiness into one of abundance, but if you define happiness, in part, with financial freedom, then why should there be limits? And what sane person would think that God wants you to suffer from lack or be denied anything that your heart longs for? And why? To build your character? To test you? To appreciate heaven? Don't countless other people, who were *not* first poor, have these things?

---

1. Neale Donald Walsch, *Conversations with God, Book 1* (New York: Putnum, 1996), 166.

And for good measure, here are more beliefs you'd likely possess if you already had abundance and that may resonate for you, but like the other beliefs, they're purely optional:

* *Everything I touch turns to gold.*
* *I'm brilliant, clever, and tuned in to trends.*
* *I have a lot to offer the world.*
* *I've always been "lucky."*
* *I'm a money magnet.*
* *I was born to thrive.*
* *I'm inclined to succeed.*

Make your belief lists for each of your dreams as creative and as long as you can, working with what feels good and right for you. If you feel as though you're drawing a blank about what your beliefs would be after you've achieved success in changing your life in the desired area, then, alternatively, let your starting point be naming the beliefs of others who have already achieved what you wish to achieve, like Sir Richard Branson, Gandhi, Lady Gaga, or whoever your role model(s) might be.

A NOTE FROM THE UNIVERSE

When it comes to "having it all," many fine, young souls take issue with the word "have." They're concerned about the concept of ownership. Their soul is taunted with guilt for the pleasure it derives from material things. And they quiver at the thought of others having less than they have.

Of course, such righteous and selfless thoughts are a significant contributor to the creation of lack in a world of endless abundance, but they'll learn.

Kids!
The Universe

P.S. There's more than enough for everyone—trust me.

Install Those Beliefs

Your beliefs are a function of your perspectives on life; they are your worldview. Normally, they assemble themselves around your experiences. Beliefs are, in short, your opinions of the moment. To change them, change your experiences. To change your experiences, *change your behavior*! Stop basing your behavior on the world around you, which simply perpetuates more of the same kind of experiences you've already been having. This is why the rich get richer, the poor get poorer, and those stuck in the middle stay stuck in the middle. People generally, and often unwittingly, manifest their life circumstances; then they form opinions and draw conclusions, which creates their beliefs, which triggers similar thoughts that lead to similar circumstances, which dictates subsequent behaviors and a reinforcement of the originating beliefs! Break the cycle by changing how you react to the world around you. Act in ways that imply that *you know* things are changing, in spite of the fact that at first, nothing seems to have changed. We already talked about such behavior— begin acting "as if"! Only now, act *as if* the beliefs you specified above are already yours.

It's easy! You just have to give it some time, maybe even months, heaven forbid a few years, but the changes *will* follow, and I can assure you that from my perspective today, however long the wait, it'll be worth it.

The new cycle goes as follows: in spite of what you have so far manifested in your life, beginning with your new beliefs, *start changing your behavior*. This will trigger new thoughts that will eventually manifest new circumstances (it's the law). Witnessing the new circumstances will cause more new beliefs to begin assembling and aligning with your dream, from which new thoughts and more actions will follow, supporting your new experiences and behaviors and installing your new beliefs. It's easy! You just have to give it some time, maybe even months, heaven forbid a few years, but the changes *will* follow, and I can assure you that from my perspective today, however long the wait, it'll be worth it.

If someone told me eleven years ago, when I was anxious and even desperate for change, that within a *few years* my life would begin soaring, I would have felt defeated and borderline devastated! Years? But my *thoughts become things*! *Years?* You have to be kidding! I WANT IT ALL NOW! I'll bet you know this feeling. Yet when dreams do start coming true, as has been said by countless others, they are always better, more fun, richer, cooler, sexier, and happier than you could have even imagined when you first set out for change. In fact, my life is so much fun today, and has been for a long time now, that knowing what I now know, virtually *any* wait would have been worth it. If I knew how good things would get and how awesome it is to be living my life now, even ten or twenty years would be a pittance to pay for the grand time I'm now having. *A pittance!*

This doesn't mean you'll have to wait ten or twenty years or even one or two years! Change could happen for you much faster than it happened for me. Look around at some of today's success stories—people for whom overnight change was their ticket. It may be yours as well. I'm just saying be patient. It's coming. And when it arrives, it'll be so fantastic that the wait will seem short, no matter how long you actually had to wait.

To install the beliefs that you've listed, act *as if* they're already yours. This simply means continuing with the abundance example—acting as if you are worthy; acting as if you know there's enough for everyone; acting as if you know you're an unlimited being of light for whom all things are possible; acting as if you know you can reach more people when surrounded by wealth and abundance; acting as if you know you live on the plane of manifestation as a "matter manipulator," an adventurer by birth who can have, do, and be anything you want; acting as if you know that you're a child of the Universe, for whom all things are possible. How? Specifically—and these can each take on dozens of forms—splurging, pretending, playing, laughing, relaxing, and "buying the shoes." A few positive gestures a day will change your beliefs—and your life—profoundly.

A Note from the Universe

The odd thing about the often long and lonely path of life
is that when you get to the end of it and look back,
you'll find that it was neither of these.

Swoosh!
The Universe

My Game Playing and Belief Installing

So there I was, circulating my accountant's résumé and writing free "Monday Morning Motivators," when it came time for my sympathy interview. I didn't have a suit; for ten years I went to work in T-shirts and shorts. So I went out and decided to make a little demonstration with an act of faith that would imply that "my life is taking off." I didn't just go to the local department store for any old suit but to a brand-new Saks Fifth Avenue store in Orlando, the first of its kind in central Florida and the most expensive department store in the land. In the men's department, I was fitted for and then purchased one of their most expensive navy blue suits. And that's not all.

The salesman chatting with me had asked what I did for a living. Dang! I didn't want to tell him nothing, or that I didn't know, or that I had just closed my business—which would only serve to perpetuate my life funk—so I slowly looked him in the eye, thought of a million possible replies, and then settled on "I'm a speaker." It was kind of true . . . because I do "speak," right? Plus, I had already joined Toastmasters and I saw speaking as a possible direction my life might go in. was speaking of a "reality" to come, even though nobody would have ever called me a "speaker" back then. Then he upped the ante by exclaiming, "Oh, then you need the best shoes in the house!" Double dang! True, I needed shoes to go with my new suit, but I was already feeling a huge pinch for what I was shelling out for the suit! I wasn't going to back down, though, and as if spending a few thousand dollars on a suit wasn't enough, I also bought "the best shoes in the house" and played out my act of faith!

Beyond that, in spite of being frugal around the home, when it came time for taking a vacation I stayed at a five-star hotel. I didn't stay for two weeks, of course—just a long weekend. And somewhat regularly, I'd allow little splurges to remind myself who I really was, show the Universe the direction I planned on going in, and pull my thoughts and thinking out of poverty conscious-ness, which is where they were much of the time. When I was frugal, I saw myself behaving in ways that weren't serving me, but I simply wasn't able, at that point, to totally scrap my old belief system and say, "Hey, be fearless." So I worked with it; I did what I could with what I had, playing both ends to the middle (love that phrase), thereby changing my experience by first changing my actions and eventually aligning my beliefs with the life of my dreams.

And remember, as I shared earlier, there are lots of acts of faith that do not require spending money.

A NOTE FROM THE UNIVERSE

Would you believe that there are some people who actually think they can change their life through "pretending it better"?

Yep! And we call them Masters.

In awe of you,
The Universe

P.S. Sure beats pretending nothing is happening. Ha!

What About When You Really Do Have Issues?

Now, I've claimed that in hindsight there was nothing wrong with me, and that the train of my life hadn't wrecked—it was only changing tracks. I wasn't perfect by any stretch, but you might now be thinking that the reason I was able to apply all I've taught you so far and meet with the successes I later experienced was because my life already was on track. If so, you may then be wondering whether or not my one-two approach for aligning your beliefs would still have worked if there *actually had been* some invisible limiting beliefs that were keeping me from achieving my dreams.

My Fear of Flying

When I was twenty-five years old, based in Riyadh, Saudi Arabia, and working for PW, I'd already literally flown around the world a number of times, often on the most rickety airlines you've ever heard of, and sometimes on ones you probably haven't heard of— with some taking off and landing on grass runways! Yet through it all, I remained absolutely fearless. I loved flying!

Then one day when I was flying on Delta Air Lines somewhere over Kansas, seven miles high, we hit turbulence. Nothing too terrible, really. Likely the kind of turbulence you've probably flown through yourself. Well, sitting by the window, I looked straight down during the bumps and was overcome by a *terror* that no words can describe. If you've yet to experience terror, I can assure you it's like nothing else in the pantheon of human emotions. And mine, being summoned by some mysterious irrational fear, wasn't something I could get a grip on. It was profound, and no amount of logic would free me from it.

From that moment on, flying became my nemesis. And on future flights, with the slightest sign of turbulence, and sometimes for no reason at all, my hands would grip the armrests and my knuckles would whiten, my heart would race, and I'd want to desperately grab the person next to me and ask, "Did you feel that? Are you scared too? Do you think we're going to make it?"

In a roundabout way and unintentionally following the advice I've given so far, I followed my two-step formula for aligning myself with my desire of flying fearlessly.

First, I Identified the Beliefs that a Fearless Flyer Would Have.

Drawing upon my spiritual *and logical* insights, I made lists:

- *Nobody dies before their time.* There are no accidental deaths, not even from the most bizarre and freakish "accidents." You do not "go" until it is indeed your time.
- *There's no such thing as death—certainly not as we've typically thought of it.* It's just the changing of awareness. When we leave here, it's my view that we "appear," for lack of a better word, somewhere else, with the same mind, the same insights, the same reasoning and rationale and beliefs and loves and dislikes that we possessed on earth before we left.
- *If and when I die, it's going to be because my greater self saw it as the ideal time.* Why would I, with my limited flesh-based perspective, want to override such a lofty decision?
- *Flying is far safer than driving; statistically, it's the safest way to travel.* I'd remind myself that planes virtually never crash, and even when they do, not everybody always dies!

These thoughts gave me comfort. I would use statistics, facts, and my own spiritual perspectives to remind myself of these truths, to seed within myself beliefs that would ward off my new fear of flying.

Was that enough? I wanted it to be enough! I may have wished it were enough! But as I've already spelled out, it's rarely (if ever) enough to just know about the truth to effect life changes. You must also live it and embody it—make it your own experience.

Second, I Installed Those Beliefs.

The way I installed my beliefs was twofold.

* *I refused to dwell on the problem. I refused to tell anyone, other than my immediate family, of my fear.* Doing so would have reinforced and perpetuated the belief in my "issue." Even when I spoke to my family about it, it was usually in passing, and I'd never allow there to be a big discussion. This isn't always easy, considering that when we go through trauma, whether it's intense fear, a broken heart, or bankruptcy, our instinct (or at least mine) is to tell the whole world what we're going through.

  I remember once walking through a grocery store after a relationship broke up due to a bit of a scandal, and wanting to grab a compassionate-looking older woman near me and say, "Do you know what my girlfriend just did?" We want sympathy. We want consoling. We want someone else "to get" what we're going through. But if we go overboard talking about our trials and tribulations, we risk lingering in our sorrows or, worse, *bringing about more of the same in the future*, as these lingering thoughts rearrange the circumstances of our lives to become more things. Keeping quiet most of the time worked for me; you might want to talk about it a bit more with family, counselors, or therapists. You have to be your own judge as to how much talk is healthy and how much should be kept quiet.

* *The other thing I did to help install these beliefs and ward off my fear of flying was to never decline the opportunity to fly somewhere.* I only flew a couple of times a year at that time,

but even if it was a short trip, I wouldn't allow myself to get out of it by taking a car, train, or bus. I was going to fly. I had to. It was my responsibility to act as if I was not afraid of flying.

You just need to know where you want to go and couple it with your growing knowledge of the mechanics of this reality and *behave accordingly*.

It took about *five years* to get entirely over that irrational fear, but the point of this story is that to this day, I still can't tell you why I went through that or what exactly was "wrong with me," although any such irrationality is clearly based upon underlying, tangled, invisible, and limiting beliefs about ourselves and our lives. And all this evidences that *you* needn't know what might be wrong with you or how you got where you are today in order to deliberately move forward and start creating life changes now. You just need to know where you want to go and couple it with your growing knowledge of the mechanics of this reality and *behave accordingly*.

For Extra Credit

There's another kind of intermediary step that I like to use for installing new beliefs, once you've identified what they would ide-ally be (the first step). Swish these beliefs around in your head when you're falling asleep, driving to work, cooking breakfast, cleaning the dishes, exercising, or doing whatever else you do. Try them on for size. See their validity, their truth: "*Yes*, I *am* an eternal being of light; *yes*, I *am* capable of all things; *yes*, my *thoughts become things*; and *yes*, me having mine doesn't stop others from having theirs." Juggle these thoughts in your head with all your others so that you see their clarity, truth, and brilliance.

Inundating yourself with truth and new beliefs to make them become self-evident and a natural part of your default worldview reminds me of *Jonathan Livingston Seagull*, the book by Richard Bach I previously mentioned. It's a story about a little seagull, Jonathan, who wants more from life than scurrying around looking for food. In part 2 of the book, the young seagull meets a wise gull named Chiang who has mastered flying at the speed of thought and can vanish and appear anywhere in the flicker of an instant and does so in front of Jonathan.

Jonathan tells Chiang, "I want to learn to fly like that." And the wise Chiang replies, "To fly as fast as thought, to anywhere that is, you must begin by knowing that you have already arrived."[2] So little Jonathan goes to the seashore and sits there contemplating this, thinking on the fact that he has already arrived. He also ponders all else that the elder gull had taught him, including that all gulls had been made in the image of the great gull himself (understanding shall set you free).

The trick, according to Chiang, was for Jonathan to stop seeing himself as trapped inside a limited body that had a forty-two-inch wingspan and performance that could be plotted on a chart. The trick was for Jonathan to know that his true nature lived, as perfectly as an unwritten number, everywhere at once across space and time.[3]

And so after days and days of not budging one inch, Jonathan suddenly perks up, opens his eyes, and says, "Why, *it's true*! Of course, I'm unlimited, made in the likeness of the great gull him-

---

2. Richard Bach, *Jonathan Livingston Seagull* (New York: HarperCollins, 1972), 34.

3. Ibid., 35

self!"[4] And as he says these words, he instantaneously vanishes and appears on a distant shore of a distant planet. The epiphany was so great and understood at such a deep level that suddenly his desire alone transported him to the distant beach.

This is a story of spontaneous illumination, and while told around the circumstances of a fictitious bird, you know well that it's happened to *you* all your life. It happens whenever you begin wondering about something, thinking about it from every angle, and suddenly, with a burst of insight, you have your answer. This is what you can use for *really getting* the truths of life, particularly the empowering truths that will grease the wheels of creating meaningful life changes. And it can be sparked by this swishing around of new, empowering ideas in your mind that are in alignment with the life of your dreams, until the day dawns that they're integral to your very existence and at the heart of your very modus operandi.

You don't have to read books to gain this knowledge, nor do you have to hear it on the news or from other people. We all have access to our greater self, to that "other part" of us, the Universe— to everywhere, always, at once, remember? Spontaneous illumination, suddenly grasping a deep truth that had previously eluded you, is available for those who use their minds and seek it, dwelling upon the greater truths that they want to embody and express. Begin by embracing these desired beliefs with your mind, rationally and logically, to ultimately reveal their truth. And, of course, all this can be hastened and facilitated with action—moving in the general direction of your dreams, demonstrating your newfound wisdom, acting the part of the enlightened, successful, happy master. Take baby steps. Act *as if.*

---

4. Ibid., 35.

A Note from the Universe

An enlightened soul is not one to whom truth has been revealed
but one who has summoned it. And not just when they've been
driven by pain but also when life's seas were as calm as glass.

Land ho!
The Universe

P.S. You do have to admit it's kind of handy that way, pain.
Just worked out like that. Honest. Point being, one needn't wait for
it to ask some new questions.

Giving and Tithing

One final thought for aligning your beliefs with the life of your dreams is about giving. I'm often asked about my take on giving and tithing, "Is this the way to abundance? Is this something we're supposed to do?"

There are no *supposed-tos*, just as there are no *shoulds*, and you can have wealth and abundance without giving a penny to anyone—although, as a demonstration on this plane of manifestation, apart from the sheer joy of giving, generosity *can* literally summon more to the giver.

Predictably, however, with many spiritual philosophies encouraging charity and promising spiritual and even financial rewards for those doing the giving, there's the assumption that some type of judgmentally based reward system is in place, perhaps mandated by a god who looks down favorably on those who give and says, "Oh, that was really nice of you. I'm going to give *you* more as a thank-you present." But there is no god "out there" passing such judgment based on your behavior, which implies *favoring* some folks more than others. Divine Intelligence is too big to play favorites—to not see the magnificence in everyone, always, no matter what kind of day, year, or life they're having! Any such judgments would not only be unfair and thus unloving (some folks simply might not be in a position to give yet), but they'd get in the way of our own thoughts becoming the things and events of our lives! The real reason giving *is* powerful is because it's a *physical act* put "out there" on this plane of manifestation that's synonymous with thinking, saying, and believing "*I am provided for.*"

Every time you give, whether it's your time, your compassion, or your financial abundance, you're saying, in no uncertain terms, "I am provided for." Let's be honest. If you felt that whatever you gave made you intrinsically and permanently less—less in terms of your time, compassion, or wealth or somehow as a person—you'd give less, *if anything at all*, from that day forward. It would literally mean survival, to keep yourself "afloat" and not squander your resources. You couldn't *afford* to! But that's not how you feel. Being the spiritual beings we are, we naturally sense life's abundance, and when we give, it typically comes from a place of "That's OK. Enjoy this gift. I'll get more." And that sentiment— that feeling and thought—is why and how you will be rewarded, because it's this sentiment that will be made manifest for you, as you have demonstrated the belief that you *are* provided for. You'll be magically predisposed to situations in which more will be given to you, as those sentiments and thoughts of yours become more things of yours.

**Every time you give, whether it's your time, your
compassion, or your financial abundance, you're saying,
in no uncertain terms, "I am provided for."**

As I said in the last chapter, gratitude is powerful because it's synonymous with thinking, saying, and believing, "I have received." But giving is even stronger because it requires a *physical demonstration.*

Of course, gratitude and giving need not be mutually exclusive! Do both when you want more—of anything! But giving requires action, and action not only speaks loudly to life's magic, but, as I've been saying, it also serves to install new, corresponding, supportive beliefs, which will generate their own thoughts, and those will generate their own manifestations. This is why I'm always on the lookout for opportunities to give (and you can be too), whether gifts, charitable donations, and tips or attention, support, love, and friendship. As you give in these ways, they will be given to you.

Finally, for gratitude and/or giving to be as fruitful as possible (and by now it should go without saying), you must have dreams *and* be acting on them.

Moving Mountains

Your thoughts do the work; they become the things and events of your life, as long as you're showing up every day with the baby steps. But it's your beliefs that allow you, or prevent you, from thinking your thoughts. Working with your beliefs by aligning them with your dreams is how to get your thoughts, and then all else, to follow suit. In this sense, working with your beliefs comes first when it comes to leveraging the Universe and engaging life's magic. With minimal effort, by first identifying beliefs that would support you and then acting with faith as if they were yours, mountains will move, challenges will subside, and your dreams will start coming true.

——————— Summary Points ———————

* Our thoughts shape our lives, but our beliefs shape our thoughts. To fast-track change, first work with your beliefs, which will in turn shape your thoughts and then your life.
* You needn't assume anything is wrong with you just because you don't yet have what you've always wanted—and for the record, nothing is wrong with you!
* You don't have to know how you got where you now are in life in order to know how to blast forward. In the simplest of terms, leveraging the Universe and engaging life's magic boils down to:
  * Defining what you want in terms of the end result
  * Taking action toward that end result
* The only thing that stands between you today and living the life of your dreams tomorrow are the thoughts, words, and actions you choose between now and then.
* Aligning your beliefs with the life of your dreams comes when you:
  * Step One: Identify the beliefs that would serve you.
  * Step Two: Install those beliefs by acting *as if* they are already yours.
* To jump-start the installment of your new beliefs, dwell upon them and focus on the brilliance of their truth so they can quickly become part of your "default" worldview.
* Invisible limiting beliefs, even if possessed, need not ever be discovered to navigate beyond them.
* Giving and tithing are "rewarded" because they are physical demonstrations synonymous with thinking and believing that you are, and will be, provided for.

------- SUGGESTED EXERCISE -------

Aligning New Beliefs with a Dream

With a dream in mind:

1. Think of or list the beliefs that would facilitate its manifestation, or think of someone who's already achieved what you'd like to achieve and enumerate the beliefs that likely made their success possible.

2. Act *as if* the beliefs listed above are now your own. To ease into this, first think of or list things you can do now that would imply that some of those beliefs are already yours.

3. Begin performing your acts of faith on a regular basis, perhaps scheduling a few per week in advance.

   Repeat this exercise for each of your most important dreams.

6

STEP SIX:

ENGAGE THE MAGIC

I have it on good authority from my zoologist friends that there's never ever been a mama duck overheard telling her babies, "OK, we've got a stream to cross. LINE UP!" And the reason, beyond the absurdly obvious, is because ducks simply don't behave this way. If the mama duck had to wait for her ducklings to all line up, the stream would *never* get crossed. Knowing this instinctively, instead of waiting for her ducks to line up, mama just goes! Then *and only then* do her baby ducks scramble and follow in line.

> **"Starting" is a *physical demonstration*, the ultimate *act of faith* that leverages the Universe and engages life's magic because it says, "I am on my way, and I intend to finish!"**

It's the same with the Universe and life's magic. Our "ducks" do not, cannot, and will not ever line up—*until we go*! Which means that when we have a journey before us, we need to just go, even when our ducks are *not* all lined up. Waiting is a nonstarter. By going, however, your ducks are summoned. "Starting" is a *physical demonstration*, the ultimate *act of faith* that leverages the

Universe and engages life's magic because it says, "I am on my way, and I intend to finish!" And with that kind of heartfelt expression on the plane of manifestation, we literally *summon* whatever we'll later need in order to complete the journey.

A NOTE FROM THE UNIVERSE

If you just start dancing, I can assure you,
by the powers vested in me (more than you could ever imagine),
the music will be added, as will the dancing partners,
the giant disco ball, and whatever else you like.

But I must warn you, "start" is not to be confused with "start,
and then stop to see if anything happens." Nope, that's "I'm scared, tired,
and not sure what I really want."

I mean "start" as in "never stop, never look back, because even if I
make a 'mistake,' at least I still get to dance."

Do your thing; then I'll do mine.

Cha, cha, cha,
The Universe

The second kind of "starting" (as in "never stop") carries with it a sense of "This is going to work. Every day I'll get closer. Every day it'll get easier." It doesn't mean you can't change your mind (more on that in the next chapter), but it does mean there's no settling for less, no waiting around for an epiphany, and no more excuses.

Tomorrow Will Come with Its Own Resources

Probably the main reason people lose steam mid-journey, to the point of actually stopping whatever it was they started, are the *cursed hows*. They begin intellectualizing their progress and comparing their *future* desires to their *present* resources, whereas when their journey first began, there was an unbridled enthusiasm for their new adventure that existed without an overreliance on logic and prudence. There was the natural-born, childlike sense that everything would fall into place, that life and its magic would embrace them, that they would know what to do when it came time to face each new challenge. Hey! What happened? The original sin—logically trying to connect the dots before they even appear. Then, horror of horrors, *these dreamers* start comparing *tomorrow's* needs, whether for financing, advertising, bright ideas, whatever, to keep their dream on track to *today's* resources.

Start doesn't mean start and then stop. It means you keep going, that each day is another start, no matter how the terrain has changed. And when we work with this definition of start—"staying the course"—tomorrow will come with its own resources.

Once you truly start, the entire Universe and its mighty, gigantic wheels will begin turning on your behalf, and day by day, week by week, month by month, those gigantic wheels will exponentially gain momentum until you're swept off your feet for the ride of your life. Yet if you stop yourself with hesitation and doubts or begin saying things like, "It's not working," "I feel so confused," or "I'm doing something wrong," then the entire Universe grinds to a halt. Your hesitation becomes its hesitation. Don't stop. Change your mind if you must. Change direction if you want. Adjust your sails. But don't stop.

And for you right now, it *is* working out. It always works out. Until you quit. Which brings to mind the words of my friend David Norris, author of *The Power of Good, With a Capital G,* "Everything works out in the end. If it looks like things aren't working out, it's not the end." If you quit, however, then *that's* the reason it didn't work out.

✳ TIME OUT ✳

Quitting

When it comes to "quitting," there are some important nuances here that if not addressed may cause some confusion and/or pain. The first pertains to relationships (romantic or otherwise), and the second, to the *cursed hows.*

Relationships

In any adventure that includes other people, and therefore other people's thoughts (that are also becoming things), you are a cocreator. This is probably the number one concern I hear from audience members. To paraphrase, it sounds a little something like, "Can my lug-nut husband, who thinks I'm all woo-woo, keep me from living my dreams?" No, as long as your dreams don't require him to behave in a certain way. He gets to decide how his life will unfold. You get to decide yours. We cannot control or manipulate others against their will. Yet when your dreams are of your own happiness, your own abundance, your own creative, fulfilling work, they are untouchable; no one can stop you.

Much more was shared on this topic in *Infinite Possibilities.* For now, however, I want to point out the obvious fact that whether or not a relationship continues is not up to you alone. In this case, "it" might not work out with a specific person, even though you didn't "quit."

But lest you feel limited here, having a happy relationship can be manifested by anyone, anytime in their life, so long as they do not insist on *who* they're having it with.

The *Cursed Hows*

The *cursed hows* are a tricky bunch, often disguised as dreams themselves. For instance, if you want to live in wealth and abundance and you decide this could best be achieved by writing a bestseller, instead of your book being just one door you knock on, it becomes, in your mind, *how* your dream will come true. Thinking about your book and working on it day in and day out, you begin dreaming of it hitting the big time—to the point that it becomes your sole focus and aim as you lose sight of wealth and abundance. Right away, you're off track to your true, originating aim of abundance. Then, overburdened with the weight of the world on your shoulders for having to churn out a bestseller, you recall, "How could you say it didn't work out, unless you quit?" and throw yourself back into your writing, swearing to never surrender until your book lands you on every daytime television talk show. See?

A NOTE FROM THE UNIVERSE

How can you know that something hasn't worked out . . .
unless you've quit?

Aha!
The Universe

P.S. It's working out; you're getting closer; it's getting easier; and you've been looking really fantastic lately.

We've already said that you need to do all you can, with what you have, from where you are to do your part in leveraging the Universe and engaging life's magic. Writing one book and hinging everything on it does not fit the bill. In this scenario, you could harmlessly quit the book, once it was no longer fun, while not quitting on wealth and abundance, as you find more doors to knock on. Got it?

* * *

Tomorrow will come with its own resources. Your thoughts today will become your manifestations of tomorrow, and whatever seen or unforeseen resources necessary for their manifestations will be part of the package. That greater part of you, the Universe, is well aware of your future needs, and you will be provided for. Even your local mortgage company works on the same basis. You don't go to a bank for a home loan because you have the money; *you go when you don't have the money.* The mortgage company knows that you'll have income in the future, that this is where their payments will come from, and this is why they're willing to take a risk on you. Certainly you can take those same "risks" on your dreams, counting not on a specific employer or contract but on the Universe and life's magic, so long as you continue to show up daily and therefore remain within their reach.

Taking action without knowing the outcome of your specific efforts is a bit like taking a step into the

unknown, or the unseen, and having to trust that there
will be solid ground for your foot to land on.

Faith

One of the greatest challenges to living in the jungles of time and
space comes from the fact that while our thoughts can change
within the blink of an eye, there is a lag in time, often a consider-
able lag, before we actually see tangible results. This means that
while we're waiting, we must not only hold on to our vision for
the changes we wish to see but also have enough faith to continue
with our baby steps, *all in spite of appearances*. Wow! Yet in
another sense, *that's it*! That's *all* we have to do to leverage the
Universe and engage life's magic.

And from this insight, the magic ingredient presents itself:
faith—faith bolstered and made possible by *understanding* your
life in a magical world, in a loving Universe, with unfailing,
responsive principles. This understanding is bolstered by realizing
that this is how your entire life has unfolded—so far.

When I began sending out the "Monday Morning Motivators," I had no idea how, or if, it might turn into something
profitable. But I knew that I enjoyed it because it *felt* right, and by
not making it the "*how* my dreams would come true," and it being
just one of many doors I was knocking upon, I had faith that if I
kept with all that felt right, I'd be provided for.

Taking action without knowing the outcome of your specific
efforts is a bit like taking a step into the unknown, or the unseen,
and having to trust that there will be solid ground for your foot
to land on. Yet because you had the dream *and* took the step, it's
guaranteed that you will be provided for; the resources, or in this

metaphor, the "land" will be there. Conversely, without taking the step, *it will not be there*—with or without a dream. This is key. We must do our part, the easy part. Dream and then show up—in spite of appearances.

I've seen it in all my careers. At PW I didn't know how I would survive, but by visualizing and showing up, suddenly I was transferred to their tax department! When we started selling T-shirts and gifts, we had no idea what we were doing, yet by holding on to the dream and showing up, each day came with its own answers, even when the day before things might have looked rather bleak. To this day, when writing the daily *Notes from the Universe*, as I shared, I visualize the dream of writing well and being thrilled with my writing, and then I just start typing, without ever knowing what I will write or how my objective will be accomplished, although I do know quite well that nothing will be accomplished if I don't first *start* writing. We must be the spark; the Universe then fuels the fire.

A Note from the Universe

The secret behind miracles is that the ones performing them begin without any knowledge whatsoever of exactly how they will succeed.

Yet still they begin.

When you move, I move.
The Universe

P.S. Once again, taking action saves the day.

Persistence

There is a word that sums up what I'm talking about: persistence. It might not sound like a very spiritual term, but it is to me. Persistence means starting and never stopping. It means hanging in there until you arrive. Persistence is spiritual because to leverage the Universe, it's incumbent upon you to do all you can, with what you have, from where you are. And that would certainly include hanging in there and staying the course! *That's* persistence. It's you insisting that the Universe meets you. It's you hoisting your sails and demanding that the winds of the Universe fill them. It's you availing yourself of life's magic. You cannot put a lightning rod on top of your house and then halfway through the storm bring it inside and say it's not working. You must leave it out there. It is the same when we want to avail ourselves of life's magic. Keep going. You must hold yourself out there. You must make yourself available to the Universe, because ... you never know how close you are.

Persist. And why wouldn't you? You *are* getting closer every single day. And when that becomes your premise, it gets easier, *and you do get closer*. With persistence the magical evolution of a dream's manifestation begins.

In the old T-shirt-company days of TUT, after we made a small name for ourselves, I remember some of our friends from the trade-show circuit commenting, "Congratulations! You did it! You beat the odds and made it past your first few years! What was it? How did you do it?" And I remember my mother answering for us, surprising me with the simplicity and truth of what she said: "We just didn't quit when everyone else did." She was right.

We hung in there when so many others quit. Of course, we visualized and did the things I'm writing about as well, but we also kept at it. One of the things that surprised us the most was that many of those who had quit actually had better marketing teams, better trade-show booth placement, better advertising campaigns, and better sales reps. Yet during the lean years they threw in the towel.

Persist. And why wouldn't you? You *are* getting closer every single day. And when that becomes your premise, it gets easier, *and you do get closer.* With persistence the magical evolution of a dream's manifestation begins.

A NOTE FROM THE UNIVERSE

Consider, if you will, an enlightened soul.

Does Kwai Chang Caine of the television series Kung Fu *come to mind?*
Certainly a likeable chap, meditating and all that.

Now picture this: A being so alive that his (or her) vibrations heighten
all his senses, his energy effortlessly summoning circumstances,
gathering friends, and blasting limits. Like a child on a playground
stretching, reaching, and rediscovering all his capabilities, he can't
help falling in love with the adventure of life. Wanting to be involved
in every game. Springing from bed each morning to greet the day.
Dipping his toes in every pool, stream, and ocean simply because
he can. Understanding the power of thought and then sailing out
into the world to avail himself of its magic. Knocking on every
door and turning over every stone to facilitate the swift
manifestation of his dreams.

Sure, you can do less and have more once you're enlightened.
But when you realize that the world spins in your very hand,
that your thoughts become the things and events of your life,
and that there's truly nothing you can't do, be, or have,
who would want to do less?

Have at it, Grasshopper.
The Universe

P.S. I know! How about a reality-TV series to
improve enlightenment's image: Gods Gone Wild?

The Evolution of a Dream Come True

Persistence enables life's magic to unfold through an evolutionary process, in which the doors you'll knock on in the future, the ones that can't even be imagined today, only present themselves (come into existence) later in the journey, if there is a journey! And there can only be a journey when you do what you can today, however mundane it is, in spite of not being able to see the good stuff that lies ahead.

For example, the idea of launching TUT's Adventurers Club, while it sounded rather fun the day I thought it up, had no form. It was just a hazy idea without any bells or whistles. I *couldn't* know where it might go and all that it would entail; I could only see the simple path immediately in front of me. Yet by starting down that path, it's as if *it could then* meander in such a way—*evolve*—to take me higher and higher, improving my view and presenting me with options that *did not* exist when I started out. As you already know, it took a long time for the site's featured mailings to evolve into the daily *Notes from the Universe*, which are still its lifeblood today.

If I hadn't done what I could, sending out the "Monday Morning Motivators," I find it hard to believe I would have ever considered or have been able to evolve to the *Notes*. Instead of taking action, had I simply sat around waiting for a great idea to strike, it never would have. In fact, without the experience I garnered from writing the Monday mailings, which then evolved into "Silver Bullets," even if I had had an epiphany to write from the Universe's perspective, I probably would have thought it was a crazy, arrogant idea. I wouldn't have been able to see how it could work with the humor, nor could I have given it the trial I was able to give it with my established subscriber base. But because I did start out not knowing how I would finish, with faith and persistence, resources and ideas were summoned, and the journey was able to transform itself.

All dreams coming true do so through this evolutionary process, which can't unfold without starting, in spite of not knowing quite where you're headed. This is how *your* dreams have and *will* come true. Don't be discouraged when starting from where you are with what you have seems entirely inadequate. That's both normal and unimportant! This is precisely why you need to start now and persist, so that the stage and your options can evolve and reveal themselves as you continue pressing on.

A NOTE FROM THE UNIVERSE

"The Evolution of a Dream"

Dream is implanted into brain.

Dreamer becomes thrilled.

Dreamer becomes terrified.

If no action is taken, terrifying thoughts grow into flesh-eating monsters.
Dream is considered unrealistic.

If action is taken, terrifying thoughts are revealed to be paper tigers.
Confidence soars, miracles unfold, and dreamer begins to saunter.

Either way, nothing remains the same.

Yow!
The Universe

P.S. The difference taking action will make in your life is more than can be comprehended. But, of course, this is also true of inaction.

You Never Know How Close You Are

Another lesson I've learned pertaining to persistence is that you never truly know, until well *after* the fact, just how close you are to when your dreams will finally come true. This is kind of scary because it means you could be really, really close, yet not knowing it, draw the conclusion that it's just not working out and quit— even after you had perhaps reached the tipping point toward inevitable success.

By our second anniversary during the T-shirt days, it was still slim pickings. In two years, I had drawn only $12,500 in pay. I remember thinking one hot summer day while walking through the parking lot of a supermarket, "If things don't get better soon, I'm outta here! I'm totally going to quit." Yeah, very negative thinking, but I was still doing all the other positive things that make life work. Besides, I didn't quit.

By our third anniversary, we were finally in our own warehouse space. I had an office to go to every day instead of working from my home. We were going further and further on the trade-show circuit and having better and better sales, and our sales reps were bringing in big orders from big customers. I was having a blast. I remember getting out of bed one morning, ready for my drive to the "world headquarters," thinking, *Man, this is it! I love what I do. I can't wait to get to the warehouse!* And as I thought those words, I had a sudden flashback to the conversation I'd had with myself in the parking lot the previous year. *Whoa!* I could hardly reconcile the differences in my life, and I had to really push myself to admit that only twelve months had passed, because by then, all the struggling we'd endured seemed so long ago. Unpleasant memories fade *fast*, especially when your life is kicking butt!

> **Even now, for instance, *you* may have already reached *your* dream's tipping point where success is inevitable—though this will only ever be known with hindsight, *at some point after the fact*.**

The same thing happened between the second and third year of my writing and speaking career. In one moment, it seemed I was bemoaning to my mother, "When is my life going to take off? Why is it taking so long?" And in the next moment, in the midst of a world tour and speaking for $5,000 an hour, a friend was lamenting his life and asking me the very same questions I had asked my mother a year earlier. Thinking his words sounded all too familiar, I was totally *stunned* with the realization that they had recently been my own and that my fortunes had changed so fast. Bizarrely, in both cases, *only with hindsight* was it obvious that somewhere during a twelve-month span my life had profoundly changed, although if you had asked me at any point *during* the transition, I would have undoubtedly shared more thoughts on how difficult things seemed and how frustrated I felt with my seeming lack of progress. Yet even as I would have shared those words, I was obviously very, very close to my "breakthrough"! The tipping point *had* been reached. Success was surely inevitable! But when? At what point in those twelve months did I hit my winning stride?

There was not a single night during those months of transformation when I put my head down on my pillow after a long, hard day—still of the persuasion that my journey "had better improve, or else"—and woke up the next morning having made it! In other words, even as my ship was coming in, *I couldn't see it*! I never realized how close I was to seeing some of my grandest dreams realized, *and they never would have had I not persisted,* allowing for the evolutionary magic of the Universe to morph itself around me. It's as if somewhere in those months I crossed an invisible line that represented the transition from my journey being a slog to a coast. Yet had I been looking for that line, *I never would have seen it, and I would have been at risk of quitting as a result had I not pressed on in spite of appearances.*

It is *impossible* to actually know how close you are on a journey inspired by a dream. Impossible. It's like messing with the *cursed hows*: don't even go there. Even now, for instance, *you* may have already reached *your* dream's tipping point where success is inevitable—though this will only ever be known with hindsight, *at some point after the fact.*

Be Kind to Yourself

One final point on persisting I'd like to suggest is that you be kind to yourself. Too often, due to impatience, we want to beat ourselves up, label ourselves, and say things like, "It works for everyone else except me," "I'm getting in my own way," "I'm too negative," all of which ultimately leads to giving up on your dreams. Be kind to yourself. We live in spiritually primitive times. In some ways, embracing the truth about reality goes against everything you've ever been taught concerning creating change in your life. Have patience. Enjoy the ride. Appreciate the magnificence of who you already are, all you've been through, and all you've already done. Change is optional. If you're up for exercising some new spiritual muscles, ease into it. Be gentle. Experiment. Be playful. Love yourself.

One of the reasons I've deliberately shared with you many of my innermost fears and my embarrassing acts of faith, or lack thereof, and told you of my doubts over my progress and my threats to even quit is to show you that *all the stuff I've taught still works, even if you entertain negative, fearful, limited thoughts.* Creating change really is simple, at least vastly easier than what the old-school approaches offer. You are loved, you are guided, and every day you are literally pushed on to greatness. Just do what you can with what you have, from where you are, in spite of your fears, in spite of any negative acts of faith, in spite of appearances, and a new world will be born—as it is in heaven, so on earth. Thy will be done.

More on Happiness

It's as if within all of us, there's a little invisible "happiness vial." We're all born with vials that are filled to the brim with a happiness fluid, and no matter what happens to you in life, no matter what tragedies befall you, no matter what triumphs or glories you experience, you will never get one more drop of that fluid, nor will any amount be taken away from you. It's a constant. It's always been the same, and it will always be the same. Tapping into it, however, comes from a choice to do so, from giving ourselves permission.

True happiness is not contingent upon things happening in your life. Happiness is a state of mind. Happiness is an appreciation for life itself, for yourself, for where you are, no matter where you are. Even if you're in prison right now, even if you have a life-threatening disease right now, even if your heart is broken or you're bankrupt, happiness is attainable in this instant. If you think it's a matter of successes, or new loves, or better friends, you jump onto a never-ending Ferris wheel, always looking for more and perpetually denying yourself the opportunity to feel it, the permission to be happy now.

True happiness is not contingent upon things happening in your life.

Imagine a young couple straight out of school. What do they likely want more than anything in the world? They want a home together. They'd be happy with almost anything—even a little apartment—it doesn't matter, just so that they can be together. Once they get their apartment, everything is rosy for a year or two, but then what do they want? A little house. That's what they want more than anything in the world. Then they'll be happy. Once they get their little house, everything is rosy for a year or two, until kids come along. Then what do they want? A bigger house. Then they want a house with a pool. Then they want a second house. It never ends. And this never-ending thirst for more is awesome! Unless you hinge your happiness on each conquest.

Our desires are gifts from the Universe that give us reason to get out of bed each morning. Our desires need to be honored. They are unique, like our preferences. They give us direction and motivation. The example of the young couple is not a little story about why it's bad to have desires. The point is that you are always going to have them—always and forever! It's the trait of the immortal to forever be growing, adventuring, and becoming more. In other words—and please read this carefully—being immortal yourself means there will always be things you want that you do not yet have. This is part of your blessing.

I'm *not* saying you aren't going to have the things you want today, but from this little story, you know that once you get them, you are going to want something else! You are destined to always feel divinely incomplete. This is what keeps us going. We'll never get bored this way. Recognizing the fact that you are always going to want "stuff" (including experiences, adventure, even love) that you don't yet have means the trick to happiness is learning to feel it even as you are stretching, striving, and yearning for more as you try to complete the incomplete-able you! Whoo-hoo!

A NOTE FROM THE UNIVERSE

Tell you what: if you can get happy right now, in spite of any problems, challenges, and circumstances that now seem to taunt you, I'll take care of those problems, challenges, and circumstances, as well as the "ever after."

Ahem . . . please, do the math, take the bait, and never look back.

Tallyho!
The Universe

P.S. I can hear it now: "Newbie angels and neophyte adventurers: Tune in for next week's exciting episode of The Fabulous Life of *{your name here!}, followed by an all-new* It's Good To Be *{your name here!}!"*

There's no reason to put off your happiness anymore. Find it now and tap into your vial, and then you'll have it for the rest of your life. This could well be the most important thing I've shared in this book. But you're probably thinking, "Yeah, just let me get out of debt and then I'll be happy; land a job and then I'll be happy; finish my book and then I'll be happy . . ." *Don't do that to yourself.*

You will be blessed with desires, *and therefore challenges,* forevermore. (Haven't you noticed? They're quite inseparable!) Know this and learn to enjoy the journey in spite of them, and you'll improve the entire manifestation process. The worrying and discontentedness will automatically shed. You'll be more relaxed. You'll understand that the destination is only something that makes a journey possible and that it's truly the journey that matters. This is why you want things, and it gives meaning and beauty to feeling incomplete.

Becoming Unstoppable

There's literally magic conjured up with every physical step one takes in a journey to make real what was once just a dream, and this is especially true of the very first step. Take it. Start. Begin it. The first step is always the hardest, yet once taken, all the rest are easier. Kid yourself if you have to. Really! Tell yourself that after the first step you're going to give yourself some time off. You might not even take a second. Just do something today; tomorrow you can watch cartoons, go camping, or sleep in.

Sharpen your pencil. That's all you have to do. Drive to the parking lot of the place you want to visit; you don't have to get out of the car. Print the cards, float the idea, join the club, open the account, price the trip, open the book, call the broker, ask for bids, order the supplies, ask for help, design the layout, dare yourself—and I'll just bet that tomorrow there'll be no stopping you.

——— Summary Points ———

* Don't wait for your ducks to line up before you start. Start first and then watch them scurry.
* Start doesn't mean "start; then stop." It means start and keep going—with a new start every day.
* Tomorrow will come with its own resources.
* Everything works out in the end. If it looks like things aren't working out, it's not the end.
* Faith, inspired by understanding and bolstered with experience, will help you bridge the present with the future you dream of.
* Persistence is just part of doing all you can, with what you have, from where you are. It enables life's magic to unfold through an evolutionary process.
* It's impossible to know how close you are to your dream's manifestation, so it's best to assume "very, very"!
* You may have already reached the tipping point toward your inevitable success, no matter how the physical world around you now appears.
* Be kind to yourself; have patience. You've embarked upon the greatest adventure ever devised by Divine Intelligence

and, spiritually speaking, you're alive during very primitive times. Seeming setbacks and dark days are par for the course; they don't mean that anything is wrong with you.

* True happiness is not contingent upon things happening in your life. The trick lies in giving yourself permission to feel it, even though you don't yet have everything you want.

──────── Suggested Exercises ────────

What Was Done Before Can Be Done Again

When in your life were you pursuing a dream without possibly knowing how it could work out yet it did? Was it meeting a partner, landing your first job, choosing a school or career? Consider writing in two columns:

1. *A prior dream or desire of yours that was achieved.*

2. *How it came true—the magic, surprises, inspiration, ideas, and connections that became available only after you started.*

Once they've been documented, use your successes to inspire the faith and confidence necessary to start what you now want to start, and persist, even though you don't presently know how things will pan out.

Let's Get Going

What can you begin doing and when? Exactly what areas in your life have you been waiting for your ducks to first align? What would you begin doing immediately if your success were assured in the following life categories?

* Work and career
* Your relationships
* Your home
* Your social life
* Your health and appearance

When answering the above, consider drawing from your answers to the chapter 2 exercises, which focused on the places in your life where you're doing something because you felt you "should" do it, in spite of being drawn in other directions.

Yeah, it's time. How does today look?

7

STEP SEVEN:

ADJUST YOUR SAILS

Adjusting your sails is something that usually happens auto-matically when you do all the other things we've covered so far. However, because we're often changing, growing, and evolving more than we even realize, sometimes we don't give ourselves, and our life approaches, a chance to catch up to where we are. This final step of leveraging the Universe and engaging life's magic is presented in a Q&A format, paraphrasing the most common questions and concerns I've received, revealing how others have gotten off track and needed clarity.

This is not a chapter designed to reinforce everything I've covered so far. These questions arose not for lack of exposure to the kind of lessons I've shared but for not applying them, not being honest, or honestly not seeing what was otherwise obvious. So in this final chapter, rather than try to pander to readers with a pep rally while wearing rose-colored glasses, I'll do my best to quickly get to the heart of each questioner's issue and offer a little tough love to my insights.

Not wanting to contradict my own advice, however, please don't think that being off track means something is wrong, and please don't jump to conclusions after you read these steps and think, "I've got the same challenge!" Simply let my answers help broaden your awareness of life's truths and embolden your conviction that leveraging the Universe and engaging life's magic is truly a simple matter.

You're already a black-belt manifesting machine! A natural-born creator! Step seven is to help you reexamine your priorities, be willing to see what's new on your evolving horizon, shore up your understanding of the truth, take more baby steps, and tweak "the machinery" with your thoughts, words, and deeds.

Clarity

Mike, you talk a lot about the cursed hows *and end results, but to me, the line between them blurs, which is not a good thing when the former should be avoided and the latter should be embraced. Tips, please!*

Clarity is what you want, both in understanding these two rivals and for zeroing in on what you're truly after. The trick lies in keeping your end results general, though at first glance this advice *seems* to contradict what I, and others, have said about visualizing details!

Manifesting Change goes into this in more depth, but it's a fairly simple concept. It all boils down to what you attach to and/or insist upon versus where you leave room for life's magic to surprise you.

For example, insist upon the generalities of fabulous friends and laughter, awesome health and harmony, and fantastic wealth and abundance; do not insist on the details that will come from their manifestation nor how they will come about. On the other hand, when it comes to what you visualize, get into the details, get excited, see the colors, hear the sounds, smell the aromas, *all without insisting upon on those specific details.* Imagine the red Mercedes, the specific beachfront cottage, making the year of your favorite hometown charity, but be prepared to flex and allow the Universe and life's magic to connect the dots and color in the lines for you. In terms of details, allow for even better than what you first set out for.

You can look at it like this: which would hypothetically be more important to you, fabulous wealth or a red Mercedes? Easy! Wealth can buy the Mercedes and a lot more. The Mercedes alone, however, may not add much to your bottom line, particularly if acquiring it creates debt! *Imagine* the Mercedes, while seeing it as a symbol of the more exciting bigger picture, the generality of fabulous wealth. Attach yourself *only* to the latter, allowing the right car at the right time to show up. It may be the Mercedes or it may be something better.

Clarity is easy to achieve when we narrow down our objectives to a few big-picture visions.

Imagining *hows* can be done the same way, without attachment. Go ahead and imagine closing the specific deal, your pet project blasting off, your speech being delivered without a hitch, your stock portfolio soaring, yet do not attach to the outcome of these *hows*; instead, attach to the generalities, the bigger picture that they fall within.

Clarity is easy to achieve when we narrow down our objectives to a few big-picture visions. It's almost impossible to create deliberate change when we're insisting on specifics because our personal tastes, preferences, and day-to-day circumstances are constantly changing, as is the Universe's ability to micromanage those nitty-gritty details based upon all our other shifting priorities and the flowing dynamics of our changing world.

❋ TIME OUT ❋

To repeat myself...

Because this is so important to understand and so easy to confuse: let your end results be general; these are what to attach to. Let the details and the *hows* be what you visualize, getting you excited about the generalities, yet do not attach to them. This detachment thereby creates far greater latitude for the Universe to find even better, faster, more fulfilling bells and whistles to draw into your life on its way to granting your big-picture wish.

❋ ❋ ❋

Being Honest with Yourself

I receive a lot of questions that reveal a bit of self-deception on the part of the questioner, who rather innocently is not getting that he or she is choosing dreams that are more about running away from something, avoiding something, or hiding from something than they are about embracing, committing, and loving, which, if seen, would radically shift their perspective and help them move forward faster and more happily than they presently are.

For example, why do most people think they want to live in wealth and abundance? Most would answer that it's to further the adventure of their life, but in my experience, it's often because they want to "buy" their way out of unhappiness without understanding why they're unhappy to begin with. They want to leave bad relationships, change careers, or have more friends—each reasonable desires on their own—yet because they don't consider what brought on their present challenges, their "issues" follow them, regardless of their varied states of financial abundance. So not only are they stressing out and wrangling with the *cursed hows*, they still aren't happy, even when their financial dreams are realized. It's this underlying motivation, and unintentional dishonesty to the self that continues to trip them up. Some examples follow.

What's wrong with wanting to write a bestseller?

Absolutely nothing! The problem arises when our reason for wanting to do something is at odds with what it is we're really after. Often, in this case, people are actually after financial peace of mind, recognition, and/or validation. They don't honestly give a hoot about writing, literature, or book sales. Typically they've never even written a short story before. Beyond the obvious fact that writing a bestseller for them is actually a *cursed how* of their hidden ends, they're not seeing that what they're really after is a way to fill in a number of empty places in their lives. If they could see this, then they could ask some new questions and explore why they feel the need for recognition or validation. They could also explore their financial situation in a new light, asking where their priorities have been up until now, why they think writing is their ticket, and what else they could do to leverage the Universe and engage life's magic in ways that would be more rewarding and personally meaningful.

Mike Dooley

I only want to be loved. Is that asking for too much?

Well, no, if that's what you really want. But if you're after the approval of others, more than their love, maybe it's because you haven't yet accepted yourself. In which case, jumping from one relationship to another, trying to feel good about yourself, never understanding what you're really after is going to make for a very bumpy ride. From most people who ask this question, I sense a motivation to run away from themselves, yet they self-deceptively explain their desires for love by saying things like, "I'm just a romantic at heart."

Really and truly, I just want my wife to be happy. That's what I most want.

Beautiful! But if you think your true motivation is to make someone else happy, you're not seeing that the reason you want this is so that *you* can then be happy. We are *all*, ultimately, motivated by our own happiness, as we should be, yet we can only control our happiness, not another's. Whether we understand and admit this to ourselves or not, hinging our happiness on other people's changing thoughts, feelings, and moods is a motivation that will inevitably go unfulfilled.

I want a divorce. Am I bad?

Not bad at all, but is that the real issue? It may be, but I've met a lot of people wanting a divorce who rightly claimed they were not happy in their married life, so they immediately pointed a finger at their partner. In some cases, however, it's not so clear-cut.

Hypothetically, what might be happening is that through a sense of helplessness, fear, or career stagnation, people wanting a divorce may have already begun withdrawing from the world around them. At first, it worked: suddenly there was less pressure. Yet over time, the withdrawing catches up with them, and as the years go by, they become more uncomfortable with the cocoons they've assembled. They sense that something isn't right. If they're honest, they'd see the paths they've taken and the decisions they've made as problematic—that they're no longer dancing life's dance, following dreams, leveraging the Universe, and engaging life's magic—and realize that adjustments could stand to be made. Instead of looking within, however, they blame their spouses, jobs, childhoods, or parents—none of which stand between them and any dreams they may yet dare to dream, yet all of which, *when believed to be the debilitating cause of their malaise*, now stand in their way of change. Unexamined and unchecked, this can escalate into a panic so intense they may be driven to regain control of their lives by carving out from it what was not even the issue to begin with.

Again, even if they're successful in forcing such changes, the underlying problems will remain, and it will likely continue to hamper their efforts to expand, because at the same time, they're still withdrawing from life.

The workaround is self-exploration, self-examination, an insistence on the truth, and a willingness to fearlessly look inward at what we've not yet seen, which can be best recognized by understanding what's really motivating us.

A Note from the Universe

The novice learns to be honest with others in terms of who, what, when, and where.

The advanced soul learns to be honest with self and discovers that "perspective" rules, yet changes swiftly.

The master, however, studies honesty in terms of motivation, where heretofore the lies have really piled up!

So what do you really, really, really want . . . and why?

Tallyho!
The Universe

P.S. Being a master can be a bear, huh?

I get you, Mike! I wanted to be working by now, but I understand the Universe has its own time schedule, and that everything is working out for my highest good!

How refreshing to hear such promising words, so long as they're not just sound bites and those uttering them are fully on board, knocking on every door as they take lots of baby steps in the direction of their dreams (as opposed to those who dream of being creatively fulfilled yet do nothing about it, except perhaps going once a month to a job interview, and upon being turned down say, "Oh well, it must be because there's something else better out there for me"). Yes! There's *always* something better out there for all of us—that's the message of this book—*so long as we do our part*. And it's true—the Universe does have its own timetable, but is that the real reason you haven't yet found employment or a spouse or lost weight? It *could* be. Or perhaps it's time "to do what you now know to do," like knocking on more doors. Only you know when you're covering up any setbacks and disappointments with what I will call spiritual clichés.

Doing What You Know

Mike, I planned the celebration party. I was even going to send you some of my winnings. Why haven't I won the lottery yet?

Similarly, are you doing what you know to do? Are you doing *all* you can, with what you have, from where you are?

In the case of the lottery, what is it you're really after? Winning the lottery—or wealth and abundance? Wealth and abundance! If you want wealth and abundance, as when you want *anything* in your life, you need to be doing *all* that you can, with what you have, from where you are. Knock on doors, turn over stones, explore income-making opportunities (whether employment, investing, attending entrepreneurial trade shows, inventing something, writing something, and so on), ask for guidance (silently to yourself and also from those who have abundance), visualize, align your beliefs, and ground yourself in truth via books, seminars, movies, or anything else that works for you. Master what's already before you. Begin and persist! Be appreciative of who you already are and all you already have. Practice gratitude. Maybe even loosen your purse strings in the name of charity. *Just* planning a celebration party and playing the lottery is a far cry from doing all you can, with what you have, from where you are.

Sure, continue planning the celebration and buying lottery tickets. I'd even go so far as to say that if wealth and abundance are truly your blazing priority, and you wanted it ASAP, then you'd be negligent if you *weren't* buying a lottery ticket every week. You do want to give the Universe and life's magic every opportunity to reach you, but don't stop there. You must do everything you possibly can to make it happen.

There is an old Chinese proverb that says, "To know and not do is to not know." This sums up the point entirely. If you know that it's incumbent upon you to do all you can, with what you have, from where you are, yet all you do is sit on the sidelines declaring, "I believe in the magic: my *thoughts become things.* I have dominion over life's illusions, and the Universe is conspiring on my behalf," then you are not doing what you know to do. This was the inspiration for the following *Note*:

A NOTE FROM THE UNIVERSE

Thinking big but acting small is the same as thinking small.

Shiver me timbers,
The Universe

P.S. And reading this while nodding in wholehearted agreement,
yet not doing all you can, with all you have, from where you are in
the days that follow, is the same as not reading this.

Retirement, Health Insurance, and Wearing Your Safety Belt

Doesn't your advice imply that setting aside savings for retirement, buying health insurance, and wearing your car's safety belt actually hasten a real need for these things? Wouldn't these actions be "negative acts of faith" that imply you will not have enough money at retirement, that you will become sick, and that in traffic, you could become a random statistic?

Yes! Yes! Yes! But do them anyway. I do! Until you have the wisdom of an awakened Christ, Buddha, or Lao Tzu and are able to walk on water and consciously choose to manifest things at will from the infinite probabilities that exist before you, don't risk your finances, health, or happiness in the name of "being positive"!

Again, play both ends to the middle. Play the old-school games, like saving for the future, but play the games that I've shared here too. Your inherent inclination to thrive in life will tip the scales in your favor, and your positive acts of faith will easily do more good than any possible "harm" stirred up by your old-school behavior.

Rely On Yourself

I have a psychic friend who has told me that this year is going to be my year! That I will likely be moving and starting a new career, and that my soul mate is now looking for me!

Whoo-hoo! Right on! This year *is* going to be your year—and every year after it too! You are an unlimited being of light for whom all things are possible. There's no mountain you can't climb, hurdle you can't jump, or dream you can't manifest! But did you really need your psychic friend to tell you this?

We've been raised in a world that has taught us since we could crawl that information, answers, and help are only a call away. Pretty good. Except why have we been told we have to call in the first place? *Why is there this presumption that the answers exist outside ourselves?* Why must we read more, go back to school, seek more advice—all exclusively outside ourselves?

To give your wheels some traction, become your own guru, start relying more on yourself and less upon others. Have your sounding boards, but don't forget that you already have all you need inside of you, including the wisdom to know what's best for you, to be all that you dream of being.

A Note from the Universe

When pondering the vastness of the cosmos from where you now sit, please keep in mind that it goes even farther inward than outward.

Yeah, you're deep.
The Universe

Changing Your Mind

For as long as I can remember, I've wanted to be a writer. I've dabbled with it in school, at work, and in my free time. But now the thought of writing doesn't inspire me. I'm over it. I'd rather find something else I'm passionate about, but I'm afraid I'm just rationalizing and that if I stop writing, I'm quitting on a dream.

Being spiritual doesn't mean making *everything* (in the physical world around you) work! And it most certainly doesn't mean you can't change your mind! Both ideas are quite unnatural, and therefore quite "unspiritual." Changing your mind doesn't mean you're quitting, nor is it contradictory to what I've shared about being persistent and hanging in there.

We change our minds every single day, especially when we're finally waking up to how life really works! Just as we physically age, mature, and have new preferences, so is this true for our spiritual maturity. As we learn more, our priorities shift, our approaches change, and our dreams evolve.

Further, when you take into account what I've already shared—that it's the generality we attach to, never the details or the *cursed hows*—changing your mind *on the approach* to a dream of yours is virtually mandatory. As we master what's before us and progress down new paths, the scenery changes and our options multiply. Seen this way, changing your mind is part of doing all you can on your determined march toward the big picture of your dreams coming true.

Simply change how you define your end results and no longer confuse them with disguised end results, and you're suddenly free to "move about the cabin." In your case, insist on finding creative, fulfilling work, not that it necessarily comes from your being a writer. Let there be lots of doors you knock on, and let all of them make sense and feel good. When the passion is gone for a particular door, give it a rest. Let it go. Switch it up, change your mind, and try something else.

A NOTE FROM THE UNIVERSE

Persistence isn't about knocking on one door until the dang thing opens.

It's about knocking on all the doors.

Knock, knock,
The Universe

Stay Focused On What Matters

I'm in a film production crew with dreams of being my own producer one day, but some of my crewmates seem to be envious of me. My successes intimidate them, and I'm concerned that as I move toward my dream, they'll do all they can to find my faults and expose them to management and investors. How do I deal with this?

Why are you with the crew? I see it as a door you knocked on, and presumably, it's logical and feels good. It's a step on the path to the bigger picture of becoming a producer and finding your place in bringing cinematic productions to market, right? Then let this be where you hold your focus—upon your ultimate end result, not the intermediary path of being on this particular crew. Don't get sidetracked from what your journey is about and why you're on it. It may even be that getting bumped from this crew, and therefore having to find another, could be the best possible thing that ever happened to you on this journey. Let go of the attachment to this *how.*

On the other hand, sometimes, especially after we've started a journey and are on our way, we begin to notice all the lions, tigers, and bears on the path, turning us into reactors, slaying the beasts, rather than remaining true to the vision and moving with it in mind.

It's not by accident that our demons emerge when we decide to move on to greater, bigger, and better things. We only think we're in peril because it's new territory. After all, wanting greater, bigger, and better things is usually a pretty good indicator that you've begun thinking thoughts that you've never entertained before; otherwise you'd already be there. Challenges are par for the course. In fact, they indicate that we *are* on the right path, and to stay there, we simply need to remember what's really important to us—the bigger end result—and keep our focus there, rather than on the distractions that seem to test and taunt us along the way.

A Note from the Universe

Have you noticed how all dreams come with built-in challenges, and all challenges come with built-in dreams?

Curious, huh?

Tallyho,
The Universe

P.S. That's why we call both of them "gifts"...
and it saves massive amounts of paper.

Don't Judge Your Progress with Your Physical Senses Alone

There are cutbacks happening at work. My boss isn't speaking to me. And I have this terrible feeling that I'm about to lose my job, while being the sole breadwinner for my teenage kids. At my age and in this economy, I need some help!

Because this is *so* worth repeating, do not rely on your physical senses alone to assess your progress in time and space, or seeming lack thereof! They are, in almost every case, blind to life's magic. Our physical senses can help you assess what's immediately at hand—your manifestations of the hour—but they are *useless* in the context of telling you where you're headed and when you might arrive. You simply cannot see into the unseen, where the real work is taking place. Using today's manifestations as such a guide is akin to crossing the Atlantic on a fabulous cruise ship from the United States to Europe and using your vision alone to judge your progress. Day after day after day, with the scenery completely unchanging and wave upon wave for as far as the eye can see, it's easy to draw the sad conclusion that you aren't making any progress. But just because you can't see it doesn't mean that you aren't getting closer to it every single day. In time and space the Universe rearranges the players and circumstances of your life so seamlessly, so minutely, that we just can't see the miracles happening even as they're happening.

A NOTE FROM THE UNIVERSE

Do you know what happens in time and space just before something really incredible happens? Something mind-blowing? Just before a really HUGE dream comes true?

Do you?

Absolutely nothing.

At least not in the physical world.

So if, perchance, it appears that absolutely nothing is happening in your life right now . . . consider it a sign.

All the best,
The Universe

And while on the subject of passing judgment with your physical senses (and at this point ties in with the earlier topic in this chapter about relying on yourself), don't let your friends do this *to you*.

When friends and contacts see us at any given point in our lives, they carry the default assumption that who you were then or now is who you will always be and where you were then or now is where you will always be. Yet they have no idea of the dreams you entertain, of what moves in your hearts, nor all you're truly capable of doing, being, and having. Still, they're usually willing to label you, not with bad intentions but for their own comfort as they try to understand you.

The very first speaking fee I received ($100 in 2001) was from a minister of a tiny Unity Church in central Florida. Twenty people sat in attendance for my twenty-minute "Thoughts Become Things" talk. The minister was present, and she must have detected that I was particularly uncomfortable (parched mouth, trembling hands, and whatnot) because a week later, along with my payment, she sent a very sweet, handwritten letter, which I received like a kick in the stomach. It went something like this: "Mike, may I suggest to you, as I do to my church members when I see them looking for their place in life, that you follow your heart and don't get too attached to any outcome." What?!

She was telling me in the most gentle and loving way possible: "Mike, I don't quite see you as the speaking type. But don't worry; as long as you consider all your options, you'll find something else that's just perfect!" I could have accepted her limited opinion of my speaking potential as my own. I could have also used my fear of speaking, combined with her professional insights, to draw the conclusion that there really must be something better out there for me. But I didn't, and neither should you.

Friends shouldn't limit friends; don't let yours accidentally limit you.

Don't Be Afraid of the Unknown

How do you know you're on the right path?

You don't! That's why you never insist on the path (the *cursed hows*); that's why you keep knocking on doors and turning over stones; and that's why, ideally, your end results should be stated in general terms, allowing the Universe lots of latitude. But let me follow this question with another one you will likely resonate with, now or at some point into your new journey(s).

But what if you feel plagued with doubts? How do you commit to the path you're on?

Commit to nothing but the end result, yet master what's before you for as long as it's before you. Remember, mastering what's before you is the fastest way to graduate from it. During the first two years of the journey I'm now on, every step of the way was shrouded in doubt! Remember, nothing I was doing could have been considered the life of my dreams. In fact, I didn't know what the life of my dreams would be! I'll also share that it very often seemed like hard work. Yet neither doubt nor difficulty with regard to your path means that it's wrong. Actually, the fact that it presented itself, that it's your path, whatever this path may be, means it's right. Not necessarily "right" forever but for today, and it will be right until more appealing doors open.

Whenever I felt overcome with confusion, I would hold my timid, frightened ideas up to the light of truth and look in my heart for my true motivation. I would look at my experiences day to day for where and when I felt fulfilled, and I'd consider other out-of-the-box options, like moving to another state, going back to school, and radically changing everything. By the time I was done reflecting, invariably, I was able to reaffirm the direction I was going in. I was never totally certain, but certain enough to keep going, which is all any of us need.

Actually, I don't think anybody can be totally certain about a brand-new path because after all, the "whims" of the Universe and life's magic may offer their own adjustments, and the next thing you know, suddenly everything is different. That's perhaps partly why, during all our journeys, we experience doubt, because we instinctively know that life is full of magic that might make our declarations and attachments suddenly irrelevant. But such doubts don't mean we can't continue to master what's before us.

A NOTE FROM THE UNIVERSE

Do you ever wonder whether you're on the right path?

Do you sometimes feel vulnerable in new relationships?

Does certainty elude you when big decisions loom?

And have you ever gotten nervous at the mere thought of speaking to an audience?

Outstanding! Fantastic! Jolly good!

So have all the other legends who have gone before you.

Walking on sunshine,
The Universe

P.S. Humility shows respect. Respect shows love. And love can only exist when there's a vision for prosperity, a belief in your own worthiness, and a sense that all is exactly as it should be. Cool, huh?
Bring on the "butterflies."

Higher Learning

Mike, do you offer any advanced material for those of us who already get what you teach?

Ack! What? The funny thing about the truth is that it's simple! I'm constantly taken aback by people who want it to be more complicated, as if they've already taken the simple stuff as far as it can take them and now need bigger challenges. My experience is that it's precisely the people who do *not* get this stuff who then ask for the advanced program.

Sure, there are mind-control techniques, hemi-sync systems, and meditation programs by the thousands, but not a single one of them is more useful, effective, or practical than *thoughts become things*. That's it! Discover it! Eat, sleep, and breathe it! Make it conscious in every moment you're alive, and once you get to the top of the mountain, while there's still time left in your amazing, rocking life, give back and teach those who want to learn.

I have a friend who started a brand-new career as a stockbroker in his midforties. He's now in his midsixties and has been wildly successful. He loves to tell the story of his success because when he was in his midforties, clueless, sweating the bucks, and starting over careerwise, he ended up joining a large brokerage firm, and they told him *exactly* what it would take to be successful in their business. They told him how many cold calls to make per day and how to conduct himself on the telephone.

They gave him ideas of how to combat rejection. They told him how many events he would ideally hold in a year to educate the public on his services, and they gave him free materials and props to give away and use in his presentations. They told him straight up, "If you do these things, we *guarantee* you will be successful. History, however, has shown that only one in ten of you are going to follow these instructions, and the rest of you who don't are going to fall by the wayside." He shakes his head every time he tells this story and says, "I just did what they told me to do—*and it worked.*"

> **I promise you, "your all" will be more than enough, in spite of any fears, limits, or invisible limiting beliefs you may now possess.**

Now, I apologize if this sounds presumptuous, but if you do the simple things I've shared in this book, none of which are difficult, none of which mandate rituals, sacrifices, or offerings—and you do them not because Mike Dooley said to but because *you now understand your power and life's mechanics*—your dreams *have to come true.* It is this simple.

You owe it to yourself, to your family, to your loved ones, to your dreams to give your all to the adventure of life. I promise you, "your all" will be more than enough, in spite of any fears, limits, or invisible limiting beliefs you may now possess.

A NOTE FROM THE UNIVERSE

Sure, we have an "Advanced Help" department here!
Down the hall and through the doors with the sign that says Help Wanted.

*Yeah, same department. We just flip the sign over so it reads Advanced
Help, because the therapy that comes from helping someone else is
one of the most advanced ways to help yourself.*

Shhhhhh ... please do not tell a single soul!
The Universe

*P.S. We also have an "Advanced Master's Program" here. Yeah, we just
flip the sign over the door that's now marked Guided Visualizations,
Fun, and Games whenever someone starts taking themselves
too seriously. Shhhhhh!*

To One's Own Self Be True

So much of the innocent self-deception I see people "slipping
up" on, causing them to not properly apply the truth to their
lives or preventing them from seeing the obvious, comes from
first not understanding or even being aware of their own motivations. If you don't understand your motivations, you're probably
being motivated by money, society, image, family, or something
other than what you really want. For example, wanting money to
take care of non-money problems will never work. You can't
mend your heart with money. You can't find career satisfaction
with money. And worse, if these are your motivators for acquiring money, you're instantly dealing with a *cursed how* (insisting
that X be how you get Y, instead of knocking on lots of doors for
Y), so the chances of success will be minimal. You need to understand what's really driving you. Very simply, if it's to further the
adventure of life, including mastering the *challenges* now before
you, well done and keep going; if not, it's time for some simple
self-exploration.

Wanting money to take care of non-money problems will never work.

At one point or another in my life, I've been guilty of every single form of self-deception I've shared with you. They're not a big deal so long as you're open to finding and addressing them. Go easy on yourself, realizing that no matter how far "off track" you may seem, the Universe and life's magic are nonjudgmental and can fast-track you back to where you want to be.

The Final Stretch

When you dream at night, are the people, places, and circumstances that you dream of real or are they just thoughts? A tricky question because I'm sure you'd agree that for the person having those dreams, those people, places, and circumstances that give them a sweaty brow and racing heart in their dreams *are real*. However, with a slight change of perspective, it's easy enough for those on the outside of the dream to see that they're also just thoughts. The answer is that they're both real *and* thoughts. One does not negate the other. Just because they're real doesn't mean they're not thoughts. And just because they're thoughts doesn't mean they're not real.

The dream of time and space—the dream of here and now—is exactly the same, except that this dream is being dreamt by the Universe, which is slowly but surely waking up—groggy, sleepy and confused—*as you and me!* The baton has been passed and we perpetuate the illusions before us by choosing the thoughts that will become the things and events of our lives. Just like a nighttime dream; the illusions that surround you right this very minute *are* real, while simultaneously they're just thoughts—*yours!*

Let me close by asking the "trademark" question that ends most of my talks, and that I asked at the end of *Manifesting Change*: Is life fair? Is it? Really? Well, if you've read closely and paid attention, I hope you just let rip one very loud NO!

Heck no, life is *not* fair. The cards of life are so heavily stacked in your favor it's a joke. You have but to think upon whatever it is you want, and it must come to pass. You live on a plane of manifestation, which you helped cocreate so that you could get your groove on and *thrive*. You're therefore vastly more likely to succeed than fail, to be happy than sad, to have health than be ill, to have friends than be alone. Isn't your life already proof of this? Life is not fair. You rule this roost. And you can have, do, and be *whatever you want*.

To create major life changes, you must, first and foremost, understand your power, which lies in comprehending its source—the Universe. And this power is channeled by your thoughts, which ultimately become things. Then give yourself direction. Pick an end result. Decide what you're going to be when you grow up, even if only in broad, emotional brushstrokes. Once you have your destination in mind, give yourself a deadline—two weeks, if not two days—to start knocking on doors and turning over stones, because the more you do, the more the Universe can do for you. For every door you knock upon, you increase exponentially what the Universe can do on your behalf. So knock away, not thinking that you have to find the perfect one, but rather, it will find you as long as you keep knocking.

Visualize every day. Come up with your own tools and techniques. Say things that serve you. Behave in ways that imply that your dreams will inevitably come to pass. Live your dreams to any degree that you can, not just to enjoy these indulgences but to declare to the Universe that this is it: "I have arrived, and I am preparing the way for more."

Be that person you dream of today, with every decision you make, every hello, every good-bye, every assignment you undertake, every conversation you engage in, every meal you eat, every morning, every afternoon, every evening, always. And never, ever, ever look back. Never stop. Never doubt. Never say it's hard. Never say you don't know, even when you think you don't know—*especially* when you think you don't know. Instead, say, "I know. I have total clarity." Reframe every thought, word, and deed of yours so that it comes from the perspective of the person you have always dreamed you'd be.

You could not be more powerful. You could not be more loved. You could not be more guided. The Universe, your greater self, is conspiring on your behalf. It wants for you what you want for yourself. You are pure energy, and your thoughts, words, and deeds send shock waves into the unseen, summoning legions to do your bidding.

You're going to get to where you dream of being, and you're going to shoot past it to places you can't even imagine today, yet they'll feel so right that you'll swear it was all meant to be. Relax now that you know the truth. Coast. Be frivolous, irrational sometimes, impractical even, because such behaviors can also be construed as powerful acts of faith, telling the Universe that you know you don't have to freak out with determination and seriousness to get what you want out of life. You're in control.

Let it be easy—easier than you've ever known. Your efforts need not be measured in time. Leveraging the Universe and engaging life's magic is not a call to work harder; it's a call to work smarter, to understand why you do the things you do, to understand that you're not alone. Stir up life's magic. Hoist your sails by doing all you can, with what you have, from where you are—this is your right. Your dreams are meant to be. Knock and seek. Ask and dream. Then move with those dreams and your every cup will runneth over, because that is the nature of this grand adventure.

From the bottom of my heart, as just another part of you, I wish you all the happiness in this adventure called life, and I look forward to our paths crossing, hopefully in the seen. But if not, I'll catch you in the unseen.

Summary Points

* As you grow and mature spiritually your dreams and ambitions will naturally change and evolve—let them.
* You're already a black-belt manifestor, a kicking, natural-born creator. All you have to do for change is adjust your sails, not launch a new boat!
* Clarity is easy to achieve when we narrow down our objectives to a few big-picture visions.
* Being honest with yourself in terms of what's truly motivating your wishes for change is the surest, fastest, and easiest way to get what you really want.
* Sure, the Universe works things out on its own timetable, as long as you continue doing all you can, with all you've got, from where you are.
* In all matters of health and precautions, play both ends to the middle; following both conventional protocols and the spiritual insights that resonate with you.
* You already have all you need inside of you to be all that you dream of being, including the wisdom to know what's best for you.
* Changing your mind is not quitting. In fact, sometimes it means taking a "higher" road.

* Never judge the progress you're making, or are seemingly not making, with your physical senses alone.
* Doubts, uncertainties, and confusion are a part of every journey, yet there's never cause to offer anything less than your best in dealing with whatever is now before you.
* You are adored!

─────── SUGGESTED EXERCISES ───────

How Have You Grown, Evolved, and Matured?

Consider how your worldviews, philosophies, and spiritual beliefs have grown, evolved, and matured recently. What are your three boldest new perspectives, and how have they—or could they— change your highest life priorities, dreams, and desires?

Consider putting pen to paper as you reformulate all that you are truly capable of having, doing, and being.

A Note from the Universe

You know how when you visualize something every day, to such
a degree that you can literally taste its reality? And you believe
in the likelihood of its manifestation with all your heart and soul?
And as often as you think of it, in at least some small way,
you prepare for its arrival? Yet still absolutely nothing happens?

Right! That's impossible!

Until next time,
The Universe